Vocabulary Workshop®

Level Purple

Enriched Edition

with iWords™ Audio Program

Jerry L. Johns, Ph.D.
Distinguished Teaching Professor Emeritus
Department of Literacy Education
Northern Illinois University

Consultants

Joseph Czarnecki, Ph.D.
Faculty Associate, School of Education
Johns Hopkins University
Baltimore, MD

Christine Gialamas-Antonucci
Reading Specialist
Chicago Public Schools
Chicago, IL

Lucy Lugones
Technology Consultant
St. Luke's School
New York, NY

Helen Wood Turner, Ed.D.
Reading Specialist
Turning Point Academy
Lanham, MD

Vocabulary Workshop

Enriched Edition

with iWords Audio Program

Advisers

The publisher wishes to thank the following teachers and administrators, who read portions of the series prior to publication, for their comments and suggestions.

Carolyn Branch
Lead Charter Administrator
Kansas City, MO

Khawla Asmar
Assistant Principal
Milwaukee, WI

Tara M. Gaiss
Literacy Specialist
Kings Park, NY

Amy Cristina
Teacher
Panama City, FL

Ann Jennings
English Specialist
Rustburg, VA

Lisa Mayer
Teacher
Houston, TX

Cora M. Kirby
Reading Specialist
Washington, DC

Megan Mayfield
Teacher
Woodstock, GA

Nancy Wahl
Elementary School Teacher
New York, NY

Julie Cambonga
Assistant Principal/Teacher
Sierra Madre, CA

Photo Credits: Cover: pencil: Used under license from Shutterstock.com/Pedro Nogueria; wood grain on pencil: Used under license from Shutterstock.com/Christophe Testi. Interior: Alamy/All Canada Photos/Chris Harris: 134 *top*; Cultura/Dave & Les Jacobs: 152; Eagle Visions Photography/Craig Love: 85 *top*; David Fleetham: 28–29; Nick Hanna: 28 *top*; iWebbstock: 76–77 *background*; KidPix: 131, 173; Picture Press/Thomas Sbampato: 126 *bottom*. The Bridgeman Art Library/ Private Collection/"Who's been eating my porridge?", illustration from 'Once Upon a Time' published by Ernest Mister, c.1900 (color litho), Thompson, G.H. (20th century): 143. Ron Cohn, Gorilla Foundation/koko.org: 74. Corbis: 100, 170; Bettmann: 15; Carl & Ann Purcell: 150; Premium Stock: 151; Joseph B. Strauss: 16, 169 *top*; Ron Watts: 109, 175 *bottom*. Dreamstime/Aero17: 166 *left*; Fambros: 166 *center*; Kalinn: 166 *bottom*; Katkov: 51; Mayangsari: 99 *top*; Mg7: 153 *right*; Nruboc: 130; Onepony: 148 *top*. Fotolia/Gbuglok: 50. Getty Images/Digital Vision: 21 *bottom*, 53, 90 *left*, 90 *right*, 91 *top*; Hulton Archive/Taber Photo San Francisco: 14; Photodisc: 9, 17, 20 *top*, 21 *top*, 31, 39, 60, 79, 86, 87, 91 *bottom*, 101, 108, 171 *center*, 174, 175 *top*; Riser/Johannes Kroemer: 36–37; Stone/Richard During: 38, 169 *bottom*; Stone/Mike Powell: 98; Stone/Alan Thornton: 20 *bottom*; Taxi/Ron Chapple: 30, 172. Guide Dogs for the Blind: 128 *top left*, 129. The Image Works/ Lebrecht Music and Arts: 142; Syracuse Newspapers/Stephen D. Cannerelli: 122. iStockphoto/Yenwen: 64. Library of Congress: 64, 106, 106–107 *top*. Masterfile/Minden Pictures: 84, 145; Royalty Free: 85 *bottom*, 134 *bottom*, 148 *bottom*. Photolibrary/age fotostock: 36–37 *background*; Paolo Curto: 28 *bottom*; Creatas: 144; Cultura/Zero Creatives: 126 *top*; Wayne Lynch: 77 *right*; National Geographic: 166 *right*. Used under license from Shutterstock.com/Gualberto Becerra: 150–151 *background*; Bigelow Illustrations: border 84, 85; Elenamiv: 98–99 *background*; emo_O: 106–107 *bottom*; Philip Hunton: 128 *bottom*; Eric Isselee: 76 *bottom left*; JinYoung Lee: 142–143; Vladimir Melnikov: 99 *bottom left*; MustafaNC: 14 *background*; notkoo: 51 *background*; Sari ONeal: 76 *bottom right*; SerhioGrey: border 76, 77; stevanovic.igor: border 106; Studio 37: 98–99 *top*; Studio DMM Photography, Designs & Art: 99 *bottom right*; Triff: 76 *top right*, 77 *left*; Vicente Barcelo Varona: 128–129; Graça Victoria: 153 *left*. Veer/Image Source Photography: 52, 171 *top*; Stockbyte Photography: 78, 171 *bottom*.

Illustrators:: Ken Bowser: 30, 31, 33, 60, 61, 63, 65, 100, 101, 103, 104, 105, 144 , 145, 147, 149. Mike Gordon: 58–59. CD Hullinger: 78, 79, 81, 83, 108, 109, 111, 112, 113, 168, 172, 173. Nathan Jarvis: 8, 9, 11, 12, 13, 38, 39, 41, 42, 43, 122, 123, 125, 127, 168, 172, 174, 175. Martin Lemelman: 34, 130, 131, 133, 135, 140. Ken Spengler: 120–121. Amy Wummer: 6–7. Zina Saunders: 16, 17, 19, 52, 53, 55, 56, 57, 86, 87, 89, 152, 153, 155, 156, 157, 162, 169, 170, 173.

For additional online resources, go to **vocabularyworkshop.com** and enter the Student Access Code VWL11S9FBQT4.

 and **VOCABULARY WORKSHOP**® are registered trademarks of William H. Sadlier, Inc.

Printed in the United States of America.
ISBN: 978-0-8215-8002-8
456789 BRR 19 18 17

Contents

ONLINE COMPONENTS
vocabularyworkshop.com/purple

- **Audio of Unit Passages**
- iWords **Audio Program**
- **Visuals of Unit Words**
- **Audio Glossary**

- **Interactive Games**
- **Interactive Word Map**
- **Interactive Unit Quizzes**
- **Practice Unit Worksheets**

UNIT 1

Listen to this story about how a girl and her father stay safe during a thunderstorm. Pay attention to the words in the color boxes. These are the words you will be learning in this unit.

A Sudden Storm

(Realistic Fiction)

It started as a beautiful day for a hike. Nicky and her dad set out on a trail that wound through the woods behind their house. They were hiking to a farm nearby to watch the farmers care for the animals. The sun climbed higher in the sky as Nicky and her father walked. A nearby stream looked so inviting that they dipped their feet in to cool off. They got to the farm just before feeding time for the animals.

Nicky pointed at a goat. "That one is so greedy. He's eating all the feed!"

"I think it's feeding time for us, too," Dad joked. The two of them unpacked their sandwiches and sat at a picnic table to eat. After lunch, they spent some more time on the farm. Then the sun began to lower in the sky.

"We should leave before it gets too late," Dad said. "On hot sticky days like this, we often get thunderstorms by evening."

Sure enough, dark clouds were present in the sky by the time they got home. They went inside to wait for the storm to pass.

"Lightning mostly strikes taller things," Dad explained. "That's why it's wise to stay away from trees during a storm."

Outside, the wind howled and lightning lit the dark sky. A branch snapped off a tree and blew across the yard.

"I see what you mean," Nicky said.

Loud thunder sounded in the distance, and it made Nicky jump. Before long, it thundered again, but this time, she wasn't as scared.

All of a sudden, Nicky saw her dog Button dash under the couch in a blur of fur.

Dad laughed. "Button isn't quite as brave as you are."

Word Meanings

You heard the words below in the passage on pages 6–7. Read each word and its meaning. Write the word on the line to complete the sentence.

1. branch
(noun)

A **branch** is a part of a tree. It grows out from the trunk of the tree.

Red and yellow leaves fell from each

_____ *of the tree.*

2. brave
(adjective)

A **brave** person is someone who is not afraid of danger.

When the cat got stuck in the tree, the

_____ *boy climbed up to save it.*

3. dash
(verb)

When you **dash**, you move quickly.

Don't slip if you _____ across the wet grass.

(noun)

A **dash** is a small amount of something.

The soup needs a _____ of pepper.

4. evening
(noun)

The **evening** is the part of the day between late afternoon and early nighttime.

We eat dinner in the _____ after Mom comes home from work.

5. greedy
(adjective)

A **greedy** person wants more of something than what he or she needs.

Kim was _____ when she did not share her big bowl of popcorn.

6. pass
(verb)

When you go by something, you **pass** it.

I _____ by the park on my way home.

(noun)

A **pass** is a piece of paper that says the person holding it can do something.

Mom has a _____ to park the car in the lot.

Permission to Park
LIC.# ATW 4137
The holder of this pass can park in the lot.

---

7. present
(noun)

A **present** is something that you give to someone out of kindness.

I drew a picture for Greg as a _____.

(adjective)

If you are **present** in a place, you are there.

Everyone was _____ on the class trip.

---

8. stream
(noun)

A **stream** is a body of flowing water that is not too wide or deep.

The water in the _____ only reaches my ankles.

---

9. trail
(noun)

A **trail** is a path for people to follow, especially in the woods.

I walk along the _____ to the stream.

---

10. wise
(adjective)

A **wise** person or choice shows good sense and judgment.

Wearing a raincoat on a wet day is a

_____ thing to do.

Match the Meaning

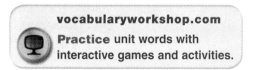
Choose the word from the box that matches the meaning in the clue. Write the word on the line.

> branch   dash   present   stream   trail

1. You might get this on your birthday. _____

2. You might see fish swimming in this. _____

3. You might add this amount of salt to your food. _____

4. You might see birds sitting on this part of a tree.

   _____

5. You might find rocks as you walk along this. _____

> brave   evening   greedy   pass   wise

6. This is the time of the day when it starts to get dark outside.

   _____

7. This is how you describe someone who does not share.

   _____

8. This word describes someone who knows and understands

   a lot of things. _____

9. This is how you feel when you are not scared. _____

10. This piece of paper says you can go into a building.

    _____

Completing the Sentence

Choose the word from the box that best completes the sentence. Write the word on the line.

branch	brave	dash	evening	greedy
pass	present	stream	trail	wise

1. Grandpa gave me his old fishing pole as a _____.

2. I want to fish in the _____ right away.

3. I walk by the big, tall trees along the _____.

4. Two mice quickly _____ by my feet.

5. I feel _____ even though I hear strange sounds.

6. Oops! I bumped into a low _____ on a tree.

7. Maybe going to the stream is not a _____ idea.

8. I know I am close when I _____ the big rock.

9. I am _____ when I try to catch more fish.

10. By the time I get home, it is 6 o'clock in the _____.

Words in Context

Read the story. Then write a sentence to answer each question below.

All Gone

Once upon a time, Red made a cake for Granny. She mixed some of this and some of that, a dash of sugar, and lots of carrots. Then she popped the cake into the oven.

Red was brave to walk through the woods to Granny's that evening. As she passed the stream, she saw a wolf.

"What's in the basket, dear?" asked the wolf.

"This cake is a present for Granny," Red answered.

"Come closer. I can't hear," said the wolf. Red walked closer. In a flash, the wolf gobbled up the cake.

"You ate the whole thing!" yelled Red. "You're a greedy wolf!"

"No, I'm a hungry wolf!" he said, dashing off.

I. How much sugar is a **dash** — a little or a lot? _____

_____

2. What did Red do that was **brave**? _____

_____

3. Which word in the story means "went by"? _____

_____

4. Why did Red think the wolf was **greedy**? _____

_____

Write Your Own

branch	trail	wise

5. Write a sentence using a word in the box. _____

_____

Word Games

Find the word in the box that matches the clue.
Write each letter of the word on an answer blank.

branch	brave	dash	evening	greedy
pass	present	stream	trail	wise

1. not afraid   _ _ _ _ _

2. between afternoon and night   _ _ _ _ _ _ _

3. selfish   _ _ _ _ _ _

4. a path   _ _ _ _ _

5. smart   _ _ _ _

6. to go by   _ _ _ _

7. a part of a tree   _ _ _ _ _ _

8. to move fast   _ _ _ _

9. when you are here   _ _ _ _ _ _ _

10. a small body of water   _ _ _ _ _ _

Look at the letters you wrote in the shaded column above.
Write them on the answer blanks below to answer the riddle.

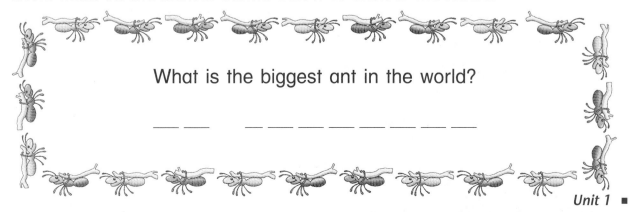

What is the biggest ant in the world?

_ _ _   _ _ _ _ _ _ _

UNIT 2

Introducing the Words

Listen to this story about a girl who rides the first San Francisco cable car. Pay attention to the words in the color boxes. These are the words you will be learning in this unit.

The Cable Car Is Coming!

(Historical Fiction)

It was August 2, 1873, and Anna stood with her mother on Clay Street. They were not alone. A crowd of people from all over San Francisco was waiting, too. Like Anna, they wanted to ride the city's first cable car. As Anna looked at the people around her, a frown went across her face. She started to worry that she would never find a space in the cable car.

A minute later, Anna heard the bell. Clang! Clang! That was the signal that the cable car was coming! A wire cable buried deep underground pulled it up the hill. The car would cross Webster Street, then the "grip," or conductor, would turn a giant screw to bring the vehicle to a stop.

People started to move, and Anna could see the car for the first time. The car was bigger than she expected, and it was shaped like a box with flat sides. It had steps down to the ground and no wheels. The windows were open to let in fresh air. Some riders could sit on a bench along the sides or back. There were poles every few feet for other riders to hold onto as they stood.

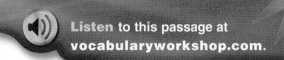
Anna and her mother squeezed into the front of the car. From there, they watched the grip release the brake. Their ride began.

In all, Anna would travel up and down Clay Street for just over a half mile and cross about ten city blocks. After the ride, Anna was so excited that she wanted more adventure. She told her mother, "Tomorrow, let's hop on a train, walk across a bridge, or ride a boat!"

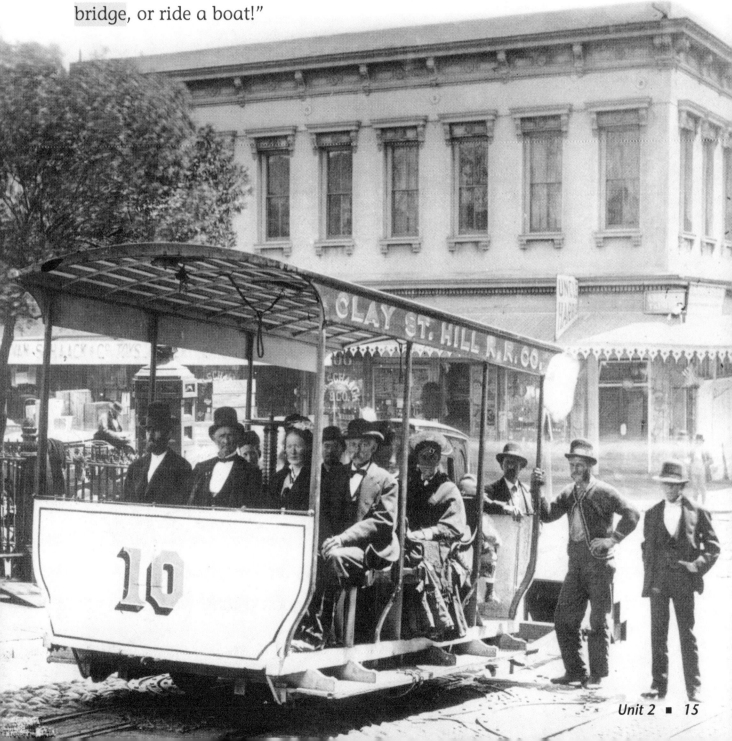

Word Meanings

You heard the words below in the passage on pages 14–15.
Read each word and its meaning. Write the word on the
line to complete the sentence.

1. **bench**
   (noun)

   A **bench** is a long seat for a few people to sit on.

   On each side of the picnic table is a wooden

   _____.

2. **bridge**
   (noun)

   A **bridge** is something that is built
   above and across water. People or cars
   can go over it to get to the other side.

   *A long _____ goes
   over the bay.*

3. **cross**
   (verb)

   When you **cross**, you go from one side to the other.

   *Look both ways when you _____
   the street.*

   (adjective)

   A person is **cross** if he or she is angry or not pleased.

   *The child was _____ when the dog
   grabbed his toy.*

4. **crowd**
   (noun)

   A **crowd** is a lot of people all together
   in one place.

   *A large _____ waits
   for the bus.*

5. **deep**
   (adjective)

   If something is **deep**, it goes a long way down.

   *The children dug a _____ hole
   in the sand.*

6. fresh
(adjective)

If something is **fresh**, it is clean or new.

I put on a _____ shirt for the party.

(adjective)

Fresh means that something is cool or refreshing.

Open the windows so the _____ air can cool off the room.

7. frown
(verb)

When you **frown**, you move your eyebrows together and wrinkle your forehead.

I _____ when I have to go to bed early.

(noun)

A **frown** is an unhappy look on your face.

When Nate found his lost puppy, his

_____ became a smile.

8. signal
(noun)

A **signal** is an action or sign that sends a message.

The red light is a _____ that means "stop."

9. travel
(verb)

When you **travel**, you go from one place to another.

I want to _____ all over the world.

10. worry
(verb)

When you **worry**, you feel that something bad may happen.

My mom and dad _____ if I don't eat well.

Match the Meaning

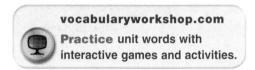
Choose the word from the box that matches the meaning in the clue. Write the word on the line.

> bridge   cross   deep   fresh   frown

1. This is what you might do when you are sad. _____

2. This is how the water is when it is above your head in a pool.

   _____

3. This is how you feel after a bath. _____

4. This goes over a stream so you can walk across.

   _____

5. This is what you are like if you are a little angry. _____

> bench   crowd   signal   travel   worry

6. You do this when you take a trip. _____

7. You might do this if you are lost in a crowd. _____

8. You might sit on this at the park. _____

9. You nod your head to mean "yes" as an example of this.

   _____

10. You are part of this when you are with many people.

   _____

Completing the Sentence

Choose the word from the box that best completes the sentence. Write the word on the line.

> bench   bridge   cross   crowd   deep
>
> fresh   frown   signal   travel   worry

1. Every Sunday, my mom and I _____ to the shore.

2. We like the smell of the _____ sea air.

3. To get to the other side of the bay, visitors _____ a drawbridge.

4. If a tall boat sails near the bridge, don't _____!

5. A flashing red _____ stops the traffic.

6. The boat can pass when the _____ is raised.

7. Once the bridge goes down, the _____ goes over.

8. I sit on a _____ and watch the boats.

9. Some people catch fish in the _____ waters.

10. The only time I _____ is when we have to leave.

Words in Context

Read the journal entry. Then write a sentence to answer each question below.

Sunday, November 7

Today was the big New York City race. The runners gathered at the bridge that joins Staten Island and Brooklyn. They looked fresh and ready to go. Then the starting signal went off. The runners began to dash over the bridge.

Crowds stood along the streets to watch. I sat on a bench with my grandparents. Others watched the runners travel through the city from their windows.

At last I saw my brother. He looked tired, but he kept going. Watching him cross the finish line in Central Park was the best part of the day!

1. Why were the runners at the **bridge**? _____

_____

2. How did the runners look at the beginning of the race? _____

_____

3. What happened when the starting **signal** went off? _____

_____

4. What does a runner have to **cross** to finish the race? _____

_____

Write Your Own

| deep | frown | worry |

5. Write a sentence using a word in the box. _____

_____

Word Games

Find the word in the box that matches the clue.
Write the word on the line.

bench	bridge	cross	crowd	deep
fresh	frown	signal	travel	worry

1. something built above and over water _____

2. far down _____

3. not "smile" _____

4. a lot of people _____

5. to take a trip _____

6. to feel uneasy _____

7. clean _____

8. something to sit on _____

9. a message or sign _____

10. angry _____

Look at the words you wrote. Find
them in the puzzle and circle them.

```
b  i  m  u  s  i  g  n  a  l
b  e  n  c  h  c  d  e  e  p
r  d  r  f  t  r  a  v  e  l
o  g  i  c  r  o  w  d  o  w
w  c  r  o  s  s  u  a  p  i
n  t  b  r  i  d  g  e  s  g
f  r  e  s  h  f  r  o  w  n
l  s  p  n  w  o  r  r  y  t
```

If you need help with a word, look it up in the **Glossary** at the back of this book.

Synonyms

*Circle the word that has almost the <u>same</u> meaning as the word in **dark print**. Write the word on the line.*

1. The children **run** out of the house.
   A. pass   **B.** dash   **C.** cross   _____

2. I use pretty ribbons to wrap the **gift**.
   A. crowd   **B.** trail   **C.** present   _____

3. Birds drink water from the fresh **brook**.
   A. stream   **B.** evening   **C.** frown   _____

4. We will follow the **path** to the lake.
   A. bench   **B.** branch   **C.** trail   _____

5. Add a **bit** of oil to the pan.
   A. pass   **B.** bridge   **C.** dash   _____

Antonyms

*Circle the word that has almost the <u>opposite</u> meaning as the word in **dark print**. Write the word on the line.*

1. Jen takes a bath every **morning**.
   A. evening   **B.** bench   **C.** stream   _____

2. The king in the story was very **foolish**.
   A. greedy   **B.** brave   **C.** wise   _____

3. Put your **dirty** socks in a pile.
   A. brave   **B.** fresh   **C.** deep   _____

4. Stan has a big **smile** on his face.
   A. signal   **B.** branch   **C.** frown   _____

5. The **person** called out my name.
   A. frown   **B.** crowd   **C.** signal   _____

 # Classifying

*Look at the words in the box. Write each word in the
group in which it best fits. Use each word once.*

bench	brave	cross	deep
fresh	greedy	trail	travel

Words That Tell About People

_____

_____

Words That Show Action

_____

_____

Words That Tell About Water

_____

_____

Words That Name Things in a Park

_____

_____

Word Associations

Choose the answer that best completes the sentence or answers the question. Pay attention to the word in **dark print**. Fill in the circle next to the answer.

1. Where would you most likely find a **branch**?
   - ○ on a tree
   - ○ in a crowd
   - ○ under a bridge

2. What might a **brave** person do?
   - ○ run and hide
   - ○ talk to a friend
   - ○ fight a fire

3. If you **cross** a bridge, you
   - ○ travel around it.
   - ○ travel over it.
   - ○ travel under it.

4. In the **evening**, you eat
   - ○ breakfast.
   - ○ lunch.
   - ○ dinner.

5. When you **worry** about something, you
   - ○ think about it a lot.
   - ○ joke about it.
   - ○ are very brave.

6. If you use a **dash** of pepper on your taco, you use
   - ○ a little bit.
   - ○ a lot.
   - ○ all of it.

7. Where might you see a **crowd**?
   - ○ at a baseball game
   - ○ on a bike
   - ○ in a deep pit

8. When might you **frown**?
   - ○ if you get a present
   - ○ if you are lost in a crowd
   - ○ if you read a good book

9. A train **pass** would let you
   - ○ sit by the window.
   - ○ ride on the train.
   - ○ get off the train.

10. A **greedy** person does not like to
    - ○ worry.
    - ○ frown.
    - ○ share.

Completing the Idea

Complete each sentence starter so that it makes sense.
Pay attention to the word in **dark print**.

1. On my way to school, I **pass** _____

   _____

2. I would like to **travel** to _____

   _____

3. To get **fresh** air, I _____

   _____

4. I **frown** when _____

   _____

5. Mom gets **cross** when our puppy _____

   _____

6. When I see a green **signal**, I _____

   _____

7. If snow is very **deep**, I _____

   _____

8. A **wise** person I know said _____

   _____

9. I always try to be **present** at _____

   _____

10. I cross the **bridge** so I _____

    _____

Word Study • Word Endings

Word endings often do not change the meaning of a word. The **s** or **es** ending on some words can mean "more than one." The **ed** or **ing** ending tells when the action happens.

The ending **s** or **es** can mean that there is more than one.

crowd + s = crowds   **bench + es = benches**

The **crowds** could not all fit on the **benches**.

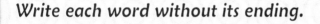

The ending **ed** or **ing** tells when the action happens.

dash + ed = dashed   **dash + ing = dashing**

Last night, a deer **dashed** across the yard.

A deer is **dashing** across the yard now.

Write each word without its ending.

1. presents _____   3. traveled _____

2. worrying _____   4. passes _____

Choose the word that best completes the sentence. Write the word on the line.

5. The tree (**branches**, **bridges**) are full of leaves. _____

6. All of the (**trails**, **evenings**) lead to the stream. _____

7. A man (**frowned**, **crossed**) the road to get home. _____

8. On the way, he (**dashed**, **passed**) some bushes. _____

9. A girl is (**worrying**, **dashing**) to catch up to him. _____

10. They see two yellow (**signals**, **crowds**) flashing. _____

REVIEW UNITS 1–2

Shades of Meaning • Analogies 1

Words can go together in many ways. Some words go together because they have almost the <u>same</u> meaning.

fast / quick

> **Think**
> **Fast** and **quick** have almost the same meaning.

Some words go together because they have <u>opposite</u> meanings.

tall / short

> **Think**
> **Tall** is the opposite of **short**.

Read each pair of words. Write a sentence that tells how the words go together. Tell whether the words have almost the same or opposite meanings.

1. present / gift _____

2. dirty / clean _____

3. frown / smile _____

4. trail / path _____

*Find the word in the box that has almost the same or opposite meaning as each word below. Write the word on the line. Then write **same** or **opposite** to tell how the two words go together.*

| little | morning | quiet | run | talk |

5. loud _____ _____

6. speak _____ _____

7. evening _____ _____

8. small _____ _____

UNIT 3

Introducing the Words

Listen to this article about how waves form. Pay attention to the words in the color boxes. These are the words you will be learning in this unit.

What Makes Waves?

(Magazine Article)

Imagine walking on the beach. You feel the warm sand and a seashell beneath your feet. After a while, you sit and look at the ocean. A boat on the water rises and falls. Water rolls in to the shore. It makes you wonder, "What makes waves?"

A wave is a moving ridge on the surface of a large body of water. Wind causes most waves. As wind blows over water, it gives some of its energy to the water. A small amount of wind makes a tiny wave. A strong wind can make a really big wave. Try it yourself by blowing over the top of a pan of water.

Because of the way waves seem to stack on each other, you might get the idea that the water moves forward. In fact, the water only moves up and down. You can see this motion by watching a rowboat or buoy. These objects will bob up and down with a wave, but they do not move toward or away from the shore.

When a wave near the shore breaks, the top tips over and finally crashes onto the beach.

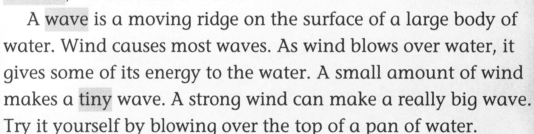

Wind is not the only thing that causes waves to form. Sometimes earthquakes and volcanic eruptions happen underwater. They can cause special kinds of very long, high waves. These giant waves rush away from the center of the action of the earthquake or volcano. You can make a model of these waves in a tub or pool. Put your arms straight out. Pull them apart and push them together again quickly. Watch how the water moves away in waves.

What makes waves? Wind, earthquakes, and volcanoes do.

Word Meanings

You heard the words below in the passage on pages 28–29.
Read each word and its meaning. Write the word on the
line to complete the sentence.

1. beach
(noun)

A **beach** is land near the water. It is usually sandy.

The children looked for shells along the

_____.

2. center
(noun)

A **center** is a place that is in the middle
of something.

My mom put the flowers in the

_____ *of the table.*

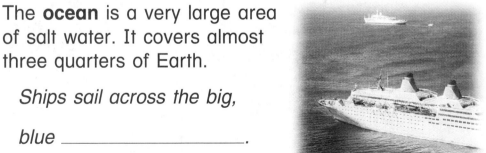

3. finally
(adverb)

Finally means "at last."

*We _____ finished our
homework.*

4. idea
(noun)

An **idea** is a thought or a plan. It is something
that you think of.

*Grandma had a great _____ for
Dad's birthday present.*

5. ocean
(noun)

The **ocean** is a very large area
of salt water. It covers almost
three quarters of Earth.

Ships sail across the big,

blue _____.

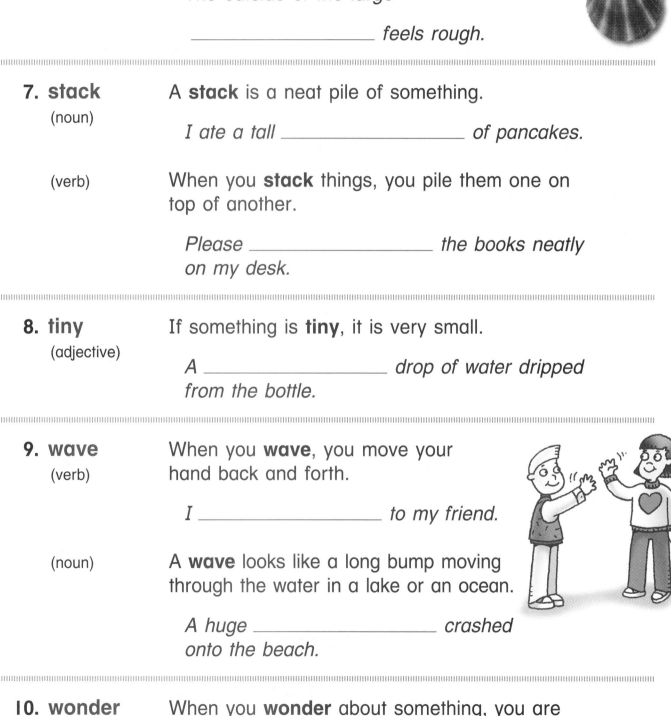

6. seashell
(noun)

A **seashell** is the shell of a sea animal such as an oyster or a clam.

The outside of the large

_____ feels rough.

7. stack
(noun)

A **stack** is a neat pile of something.

I ate a tall _____ of pancakes.

(verb)

When you **stack** things, you pile them one on top of another.

Please _____ the books neatly on my desk.

8. tiny
(adjective)

If something is **tiny**, it is very small.

A _____ drop of water dripped from the bottle.

9. wave
(verb)

When you **wave**, you move your hand back and forth.

I _____ to my friend.

(noun)

A **wave** looks like a long bump moving through the water in a lake or an ocean.

A huge _____ crashed onto the beach.

10. wonder
(verb)

When you **wonder** about something, you are curious about it. You want to learn about it.

I _____ why the sky is blue.

Match the Meaning

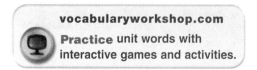
vocabularyworkshop.com
Practice unit words with interactive games and activities.

Choose the word from the box that matches the meaning in the clue. Write the word on the line.

> beach   idea   ocean   seashell   stack

1. This is something that belongs to some sea animals.

    _____

2. This is a sandy place by the water. _____

3. This is a large body of salt water. _____

4. This is a tall pile of something. _____

5. This is a plan you are thinking about. _____

> center   finally   tiny   wave   wonder

6. You might do this when you greet a friend. _____

7. You might stand here so all the children can see what you are doing. _____

8. You might say this word after you finish cleaning up your room.

    _____

9. You might use this word to describe an ant. _____

10. You might do this when you want to know why something is happening. _____

Completing the Sentence

Choose the word from the box that best completes the
sentence. Write the word on the line.

beach	center	finally	idea	ocean
seashell	stack	tiny	wave	wonder

1. I walk on the soft sand at the _____.

2. A whale is a large animal that lives in the _____.

3. I _____ how heavy a whale is.

4. Inside the shell I found lives a _____ crab.

5. There is a hole near the _____ of a clam's shell.

6. I also found a pretty _____ on the beach.

7. A _____ carries some shells in from the sea.

8. The wave almost washes away the _____ of pails.

9. _____ the children move the pails away.

10. That was a good _____!

Words in Context

Read the story. Then write a sentence to answer each question below.

A Summer Idea

Jenny loved the winter. But it was summer, and she was at the beach. Suddenly she had an idea.

Jenny began to gather seashells and sticks. Dad watched. "I wonder what she's doing," he said to himself.

Jenny made three different-size balls of sand and stacked them. She put the biggest ball on the bottom and the smallest ball on top. Then she stuck two long sticks in the middle ball, one stick on each side. She put seashells in the top ball to make the eyes, ears, and nose. Dad laughed. He finally figured out what Jenny was doing.

1. What did Dad **wonder** about? _____

_____

2. How did Jenny **stack** the balls of sand? _____

_____

3. What word in the story means "at last"? _____

_____

4. What was Jenny's **idea**? _____

_____

Write Your Own

center	ocean	tiny	wave

5. Write a sentence using a word in the box. _____

_____

Word Games

Find the word in the box that matches the clue.
Write the word on the puzzle.

beach	center	finally	idea	ocean
seashell	stack	tiny	wave	wonder

ACROSS

2. a sandy place by the ocean

5. something that you think of

6. at last

7. a pile

9. to want to know

DOWN

1. a large body of salt water

3. very, very small

4. the hard shell of a sea animal

8. the middle of something

9. what you might do to say hello

UNIT 4

Introducing the Words

Listen to this story about a family's trip to see the northern lights. Pay attention to the words in the color boxes. These are the words you will be learning in this unit.

A Midnight Rainbow
(Informational Fiction)

Lily and Jonah could not wait for spring break. All week, they talked about their trip. In a few days, they would arrive in Alaska to see the northern lights, a natural display of glowing colors in the night sky. Even though their parents had shown them pictures of the northern lights, Lily and Jonah still weren't sure exactly what to expect.

"How can rainbow colors appear in the dark?" Jonah asked.

"You'll just have to wait and see," Mom answered. "As long as we have good weather in Alaska, we should get a great show."

"I think this is the first time I'm not hoping for a snowstorm," Lily laughed.

"That's why we're going in March," Dad said. "It's not summer yet, so the sky still gets dark enough for us to see the northern lights. However, it won't be as cold and snowy as it would be in the winter."

That weekend, the family flew to Fairbanks, Alaska. There was some winter snow still on the ground, but skies were clear. Even in March, it felt cold to Lily and Jonah, especially at night. They wore winter coats and sipped hot chocolate as they waited and waited for the northern lights. It was almost midnight when a faint glow appeared where the land met the sky.

Slowly, the light grew and rose higher. It seemed to float right above the trees. Soon, the sky was painted with enormous swirls of green and yellow. Jonah was so amazed that he could barely speak.

"Awesome," he said in an excited whisper.

Word Meanings

You heard the words below in the passage on pages 36–37.
Read each word and its meaning. Write the word on the
line to complete the sentence.

1. arrive
(verb)

When you **arrive** somewhere, you reach the
place you set out for.

I _____ at school at 8 o'clock.

2. clear
(adjective)

When something is **clear**, it is not cloudy or dark.

There was not one cloud in the

_____ sky.

(adjective)

Clear can also mean that you can
see through something easily.

We could see the rocks at the

bottom of the _____ lake.

3. enormous
(adjective)

Anything **enormous** is very big.

The elephant is _____.

4. exactly
(adverb)

If something looks or happens **exactly** like something
else, it looks or happens in the same way.

*My bike looks _____
like yours.*

5. float
(verb)

When things **float**, they stay on top
of water or in the air.

I let go of the balloon and watched it

_____ above the tree.

6. midnight
(noun)

Midnight comes at 12 o'clock at night. It is called midnight because it is in the middle of the night.

I try to stay up until _____, but I always fall asleep.

---

7. rainbow
(noun)

A **rainbow** is made of long stripes of color in the sky. If the sun shines after it rains, you often see a rainbow.

I can see orange, red, purple, blue, and

other colors in a _____.

---

8. snowstorm
(noun)

A **snowstorm** happens when a lot of snow falls.

Over a foot of snow fell during the

_____.

---

9. weekend
(noun)

The **weekend** is made up of the two days of the week called Saturday and Sunday.

I visit and eat lunch with my grandfather

every _____.

---

10. whisper
(verb)

When you **whisper**, you speak in a very soft and quiet voice.

We _____ so that no one else will hear what we say.

Match the Meaning

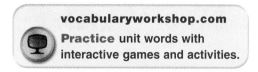

Choose the word from the box that matches the meaning in the clue. Write the word on the line.

clear	midnight	rainbow	snowstorm	weekend

1. This is a time when most people are sleeping. _____

2. This is a big storm with a lot of snow. _____

3. This is what we call the two days Saturday and Sunday.

   _____

4. This is what you might see in the sky after it rains.

   _____

5. This word describes a blue sky that has no clouds.

   _____

arrive	enormous	exactly	float	whisper

6. You do this when you speak softly. _____

7. You do this when you get to a new place. _____

8. You see a ball do this on top of the water. _____

9. You might use this word to describe something that is very big.

   _____

10. You might use this word to tell how alike twin sisters look.

    _____

Completing the Sentence

Choose the word from the box that best completes the
sentence. Write the word on the line.

arrive	clear	enormous	exactly	float
midnight	rainbow	snowstorm	weekend	whisper

1. I woke up at _____ and saw the snow falling.

2. Tomorrow is the beginning of the _____, and there is no school.

3. "We will play in the snow tomorrow," I _____ to my sister.

4. The snow clouds have gone, and the sky is _____.

5. My two friends finally _____ at 9 o'clock.

6. We make an _____ snowman.

7. His hat has all the colors of the _____ on it.

8. My sister makes a snowman _____ like ours!

9. Later that afternoon, dark gray clouds _____ in.

10. Maybe we will have another _____ tonight.

Words in Context

Read the speech balloon. Then write a sentence to answer each question below.

Hello, summer lovers! Today's weather is clear and is almost exactly like the beautiful day we had yesterday. Around midnight tonight, we expect clouds to move in. Don't worry, though. By the weekend, it will be clear and hot again.

So beach lovers, arrive early at the beach for a good spot. As you lie on the sand, put your hands in the cool, clear water. If you feel hot, just think about that enormous snowstorm we had only three months ago.

Until tomorrow, I am your Weatherwoman Wendy, with summer skies all around!

WENDY THE WEATHER WOMAN

1. What is today's weather almost **exactly** like? _____

_____

2. What will the weather be like around **midnight**? _____

_____

3. What will the weather be like by the **weekend**? _____

_____

4. Why should people **arrive** early at the beach? _____

_____

Write Your Own

float   rainbow   whisper

5. Write a sentence using a word in the box. _____

_____

Word Games

Find the word in the box that matches the clue.
Write each letter of the word on an answer blank.

arrive	clear	enormous	exactly	float
midnight	rainbow	snowstorm	weekend	whisper

1. stay on top of water   — — — — —

2. speak softly   — — — — — — —

3. not muddy   — — — — —

4. something colorful in
   the sky   — — — — — — —

5. huge   — — — — — — — —

6. in the very same way   — — — — — — —

7. a big snowfall   — — — — — — — — —

8. comes after evening   — — — — — — — —

9. comes after Friday   — — — — — — —

10. to reach a place   — — — — — —

Look at the letters you wrote in the shaded column above.
Write them on the answer blanks below to answer the riddle.

What side of a bird has the most feathers?

— — — —   — — — — — — —

Synonyms

*Circle the word that has almost the <u>same</u> meaning as the word in **dark print**. Write the word on the line.*

1. The boat sailed across the **sea.**
   A. ocean   **B.** beach   **C.** seashell   _____

2. I have a **plan** for a school play.
   A. wave   **B.** idea   **C.** ocean   _____

3. The **seashore** is covered with shells.
   A. rainbow   **B.** beach   **C.** snowstorm   _____

4. There is jelly in the **middle** of the donut.
   A. center   **B.** idea   **C.** wave   _____

5. Please **pile** the newspapers in the corner.
   A. arrive   **B.** stack   **C.** whisper   _____

Antonyms

*Circle the word that has almost the <u>opposite</u> meaning as the word in **dark print**. Write the word on the line.*

1. I **leave** home at 8 o'clock.
   A. wonder   **B.** arrive   **C.** wave   _____

2. What a **huge** pumpkin!
   A. tiny   **B.** enormous   **C.** clear   _____

3. Don't **shout** so much!
   A. float   **B.** stack   **C.** whisper   _____

4. Will the toy boat **sink** in the pool?
   A. arrive   **B.** float   **C.** stack   _____

5. The **little** elephant sprayed water on us.
   A. clear   **B.** tiny   **C.** enormous   _____

REVIEW UNITS 3–4

Classifying

Look at the words in the box. Write each word in the group in which it best fits. Use each word once.

clear	enormous	ocean	seashell
snowstorm	stack	tiny	whisper

Words That Tell About Size

_____

_____

Words About the Beach

_____

_____

Weather Words

_____

_____

Action Words

_____

_____

Word Associations

*Choose the answer that best completes the sentence or answers the question. Pay attention to the word in **dark print**. Fill in the circle next to the answer.*

1. What might you do at the **beach**?
   - ○ climb a tall mountain
   - ○ gather leaves
   - ○ dig in the sand

2. Who might stand at the **center** of a stage?
   - ○ a bird
   - ○ a baby
   - ○ an actor

3. When might you see a **rainbow**?
   - ○ at night
   - ○ after it rains
   - ○ before it rains

4. On a snowy day, it's a good **idea** to
   - ○ put on a hat and boots.
   - ○ swim in the lake.
   - ○ wear shorts.

5. If you **stack** blocks, you
   - ○ hide them.
   - ○ color them.
   - ○ pile them.

6. When you **wonder** about something, you
   - ○ don't care about it.
   - ○ want to know more about it.
   - ○ are scared of it.

7. You have **exactly** five cents if you have
   - ○ a penny.
   - ○ a nickel.
   - ○ a dime.

8. What might a **wave** in the ocean do?
   - ○ shake your hand
   - ○ make you hot
   - ○ splash water on you

9. What might you **finally** do at the end of the day?
   - ○ write a story
   - ○ play in the park
   - ○ go to sleep

10. You might find **clear** water in
    - ○ a muddy pond.
    - ○ the dirt.
    - ○ a swimming pool.

Completing the Idea

Complete each sentence starter so that it makes sense.
Pay attention to the word in **dark print.**

1. If I **arrive** late at school, I _____

   _____

2. When it is dark and cloudy, I **wonder** if _____

   _____

3. After the **snowstorm**, I _____

   _____

4. On a sunny and **clear** day, I _____

   _____

5. At the beach, the giant **wave** _____

   _____

6. When I go to the **beach**, I _____

   _____

7. On the **weekend**, I _____

   _____

8. When I **finally** go to the park, I _____

   _____

9. At **midnight**, I _____

   _____

10. The bus arrived at **exactly** _____

   _____

Word Study • Compound Words

> A **compound word** is made up of two smaller words. Sometimes, the smaller words can help you figure out the meaning of the compound word.
>
> **mail + box = mailbox**
>
> A **mailbox** is a **box** for your **mail**.

Put the words together to make a compound word. Write the new word on the line.

1. snow + storm = _____

2. sea + shell = _____

3. rain + bow = _____

4. week + end = _____

5. mid + night = _____

*Read each sentence. Write **yes** if the sentence gives the meaning of the word in **dark print.***

6. A **snowstorm** is a storm with lots of snow. _____

7. A **seashell** is the shell of a sea animal. _____

8. A **rainbow** is a bow made from rain. _____

9. A **weekend** is the days at the end of a week. _____

One sentence above does not give the correct meaning of the compound word. Write the correct meaning of the word below.

10. _____

_____

Shades of Meaning • Word Families

A **word family** is a group of related words that share some meaning. If you know one word in a family, you have an idea about what the other words mean.

wonder	something that amazes A rainbow is a **wonder** of nature.
wonderful	very good or amazing You might say that a **wonderful** idea is a great idea.
wonderfully	in a great or wonderful way You might say that a song is **wonderfully** sung.

*Read each sentence. The words in **dark print** are related to words in the box. Circle the word that best completes the sentence.*

> add   arrive   fresh   wonder

1. When I find a sum, I am doing (**arrival**, **addition**).

2. We had a (**fresher**, **wonderful**) time at the school play.

3. I opened the box as soon as it (**arrived**, **wondered**).

4. Our clothes are all (**additionally**, **freshly**) washed.

Add the ending to form a related word. Then write a sentence with the new word. The first one has been done for you.

5. **sing + er =** _____singer_____

   The singer has a beautiful voice.

6. **quiet + ly =** _____

   _____

7. **art + ist =** _____

   _____

Introducing the Words

Listen to this passage and recipe to learn how to make fruity pineapple pancakes. Pay attention to the words in the color boxes. These are the words you will be learning in this unit.

Pineapple Pancakes
(Recipe/How-to)

How would you like to nibble on your very own taste of the rain forest? One fruit that you know is actually grown there. It's the pineapple! This juicy fruit is popular and good for you. It can be added to a fruit salad or even cooked with meat. In some cultures, this fancy fruit has become known as a sign of welcome. On a tropical island, you may see pineapples on display in a hotel, inn, or other place that visitors go.

One simple and fun way to enjoy pineapple is to make pineapple pancakes. Here is a recipe. It will take you less than one hour to make and eat the pancakes. As any recipe will warn you, be sure to read the instructions carefully, and always cook with an adult.

Pineapple fruit is bright yellow, but the pancakes will be pale in color. You can put more pineapple on your pancakes before eating them. Be sure to chew slowly to enjoy every fruity bite!

Pineapple Pancakes

Makes eight 4-inch round pancakes

1 ¼ cup flour
  3 teaspoons baking powder
  1 tablespoon sugar
  ½ teaspoon salt

1 egg, beaten
1 cup milk
2 tablespoons oil
½ cup crushed pineapple, drained

Mix the flour, baking powder, sugar, and salt in a bowl. In another bowl, mix the egg, milk, and oil. Stir this mixture into the first mixture. The batter will be lumpy. Stir in the pineapple.

Lightly grease a griddle or pan, and heat it. Drop large spoonfuls of batter onto the griddle or pan. Turn over each pancake when the underside is golden brown. Cook until the other side is also golden brown.

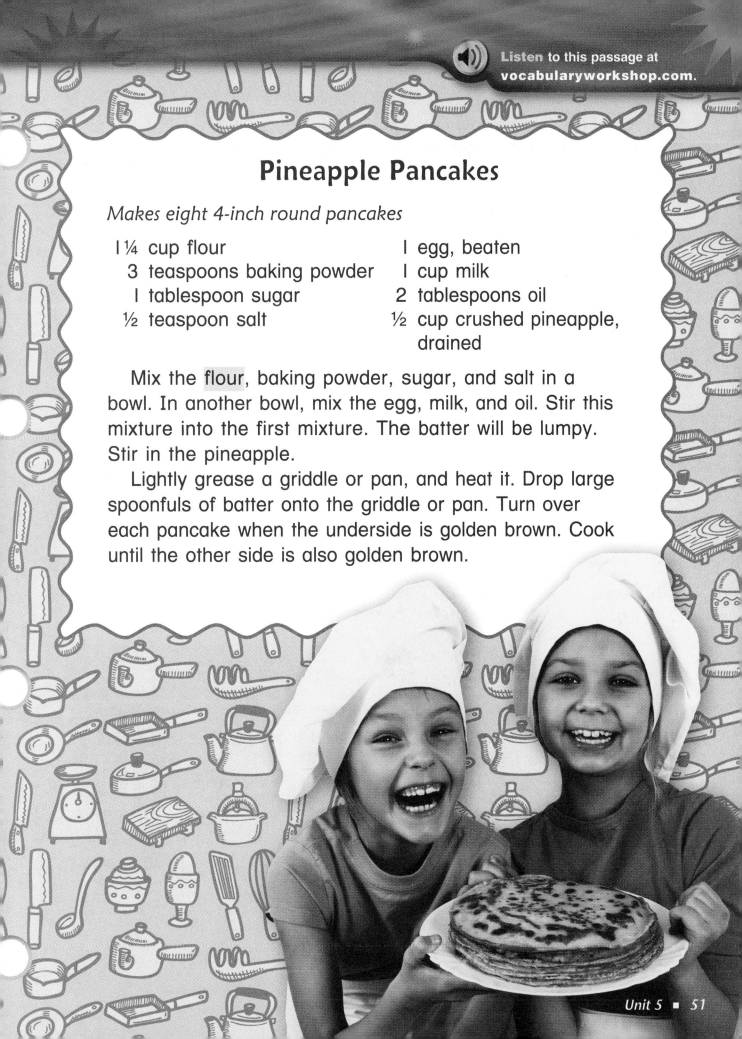

Word Meanings

You heard the words below in the passage on pages 50–51.
Read each word and its meaning. Write the word on the
line to complete the sentence.

1. **bright**
(adjective)

If something is **bright**, it gives a lot of light.

The sun is _____ today.

(adjective)

Something **bright** can also mean
something that is shiny.

I scrubbed the pot until it looked

_____ and clean.

2. **chew**
(verb)

When you **chew** something, you break it into small
pieces with your teeth.

I _____ my food before I swallow it.

3. **flour**
(noun)

Flour is a powder made from grain. It is used to
make bread, cakes, and pies.

*We put a cup of _____ into the
bowl with the milk and eggs.*

4. **forest**
(noun)

A **forest** is a large area that has
trees and plants.

Deer live in the _____.

5. **hour**
(noun)

An **hour** is an amount of time.
It is sixty minutes long.

*It takes one _____ to
bake the cake.*

6. inn
(noun)

An **inn** is a small place where a person can eat a meal and stay for the night. It is usually in the country.

After traveling all day, we stopped at an

_____ *for the night.*

7. island
(noun)

An **island** is a piece of land with water all around it.

It took the boat two hours

to sail around the _____.

8. nibble
(verb)

If you **nibble** on something, you eat it with very small bites.

Rabbits _____ *on carrots.*

9. pale
(adjective)

If something is **pale**, it has very little color.

Jason's face looks _____ *because he is very sick.*

10. warn
(verb)

If you **warn** someone, you tell the person about possible danger. A sign or signal can also warn.

The signs _____ *us not to walk on the ice.*

DANGER! THIN ICE

DO NOT CROSS!

Match the Meaning

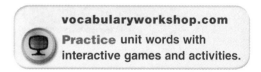
*Choose the word from the box that matches the meaning
in the clue. Write the word on the line.*

> flour   forest   hour   island   nibble

1. This is land that has water all around it. _____

2. This is 60 minutes long. _____

3. This is a place that has many trees and plants. _____

4. This is made from grain and used in baking. _____

5. This is what you do when you take little bites. _____

> bright   chew   inn   pale   warn

6. This is a place where you can stop and sleep. _____

7. This word tells about something that has little color.

   _____

8. You do this to tell someone about danger. _____

9. You might use this word to tell about something shiny.

   _____

10. You do this with your teeth to break up food. _____

Completing the Sentence

Choose the word from the box that best completes the
sentence. Write the word on the line.

bright	chew	flour	forest	hour
inn	island	nibble	pale	warn

1. The chicks sleep for an _____, and then they wake up.

2. They can see the _____ moon in the sky.

3. They find tiny specks of white _____ on the trail.

4. They begin to _____ on the tiny grains.

5. The chicks walk through the dark _____.

6. They pass by an _____ where people are sleeping.

7. Then they see an _____ in the middle of the lake.

8. They can see a garden full of corn in the _____ light.

9. Signs _____ the chicks of foxes on the island.

10. The chicks would love to _____ the corn.

Words in Context

Read the story. Then write a sentence to answer
each question below.

The Lion and the Mouse

One bright sunny day, Lion was asleep in the forest.
Mouse didn't see Lion and ran right over his nose!

Lion grabbed Mouse and roared, "I warn you. Don't
ever do that again!"

"I won't," said Mouse. "Let me go, and one day I'll
save your life."

Lion laughed but let Mouse go. An hour later,
hunters caught Lion in a net. Mouse heard Lion's cries
and found him.

Mouse said, "I will nibble on the rope."

"Don't nibble!" Lion said. "Chew fast!"

And that was just what Mouse did. From then on,
Lion and Mouse were great friends.

1. When and where does this story take place? _____

_____

2. What does Lion **warn** Mouse about? _____

_____

3. What happens an **hour** after Mouse leaves Lion? _____

_____

4. How does Mouse help Lion? _____

_____

Write Your Own

> flour   inn   island   pale

5. Write a sentence using a word in the box. _____

_____

Word Games

Find the word in the box that matches the clue.
Write the word on the line.

bright	chew	flour	forest	hour
inn	island	nibble	pale	warn

1. longer than a minute and shorter than a day _____

2. a small place to stay for the night _____

3. a piece of land in an ocean _____

4. where you might find different kinds of animals _____

5. what flashing red lights do _____

6. the sun on a summer day _____

7. what a rabbit does to lettuce _____

8. very light in color _____

9. what you need to make a cake _____

10. what you do to gum _____

Look at the words you wrote. Find
them in the puzzle and circle them.

f	l	o	u	r	c	d	h	e	x
m	l	b	r	i	g	h	t	i	x
i	l	o	p	a	l	e	d	o	b
h	o	u	r	i	c	w	a	r	n
n	i	b	b	l	e	d	d	h	x
j	c	h	e	w	c	d	f	i	p
l	f	o	r	e	s	t	h	u	p
i	n	n	u	i	s	l	a	n	d

Introducing the Words

Listen to this folktale about why bears have short tails. Pay attention to the words in the color boxes. These are the words you will be learning in this unit.

Why Bears Have Short Tails

(Folktale)

Many years ago, Bear had a long, fluffy tail. Every morning, she would boast, "I think my tail looks so very pretty today."

The other forest animals were too weak to stand up to her. Instead, they could only agree.

"It's a nice tail," Rabbit and Chipmunk would say in gentle voices.

Then one cold, winter day, Fox had a clever idea. He was famous for being tricky. Fox asked all the animals to help him catch lots of fish. Then he found a spot where he could sit on the frozen pond and put all the fish around him. He knew Bear would come by to search for food.

Fox sat on the ice and waited. Up above, the bare winter branches blew in the brisk wind. At last, Bear arrived. She licked her lips and came over to Fox.

"How did you catch so many fish?" Bear asked.

"I used my tail," Fox said. "I bet you'd catch even more with your lovely tail. Try it here. This is the best spot for fishing."

Bear made a hole in the icy pond and dipped her tail in the dark, cold water.

Fox rubbed his paws together. "Tonight, we'll have a fish feast."

"We?" chuckled Bear. "You mean *I'll* have a fish feast tonight."

Fox shrugged. "Whatever you say. You're the leader of this forest."

Bear sat on the ice for a long time. She sat so long that she fell asleep. When she woke hours later, she didn't notice that her tail had frozen into the ice. She tugged hard at her tail, and part of it snapped off!

"My beautiful tail!" Bear cried, running off in shame.

From then on, Fox was a hero in the forest. The forest animals didn't have to hear about Bear's tail ever again.

Word Meanings

You heard the words below in the passage on pages 58–59.
Read each word and its meaning. Write the word on the
line to complete the sentence.

1. **agree**
   (verb)

   When you **agree** with someone, you think the
   same way as the other person.

   *Sam and I _____ that
   ice skating is fun.*

2. **bare**
   (adjective)

   If something is **bare**, it is not covered.

   *I put my _____
   legs into the water.*

3. **famous**
   (adjective)

   A **famous** person is someone who is known
   by many people.

   Babe Ruth is a baseball player

   who is _____.

4. **feast**
   (noun)

   A **feast** is a very large meal on
   a special day.

   Mom cooks a

   *_____ on
   Thanksgiving Day.*

5. **gentle**
   (adjective)

   If something is **gentle**, it is very soft and mild.

   I gave my baby sister a warm and

   _____ hug.

6. hero
(noun)

A **hero** is a person you look up to for having done something good and brave.

The boy is a _____ for rescuing the cat from the tree.

7. leader
(noun)

A **leader** is a person who shows people where to go or how to do something.

We followed the _____ up the path.

8. notice
(verb)

If you **notice** something, you see it.

The mouse was so quiet that the cat

did not _____ it.

(noun)

A **notice** is a sign put up for people to read.

Dad read the _____ about the missing dog.

9. search
(verb)

If you **search** for something, you look for it.

Please help me _____ for my lost shoes.

10. weak
(adjective)

If you feel **weak**, you do not feel strong.

You cannot lift that heavy box if you

are _____.

Match the Meaning

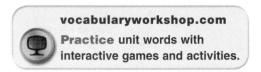
Choose the word from the box that matches the meaning
in the clue. Write the word on the line.

agree	feast	hero	notice	search

1. You do this when you see something. _____

2. You do this when you look for something. _____

3. You do this when you and another person think alike.

_____

4. This is a person who is brave and good. _____

5. This is a huge meal that celebrates a special day.

_____

bare	famous	gentle	leader	weak

6. This is how you describe a person who many people know.

_____

7. This is a person who is in charge. _____

8. This is how you describe a person who is soft and mild.

_____

9. This word describes a person who is not strong. _____

10. This word describes something that is not covered.

_____

Completing the Sentence

Choose the word from the box that best completes the
sentence. Write the word on the line.

agree	bare	famous	feast	gentle
hero	leader	notice	search	weak

1. The town put up a _____ about the big party.

2. Everyone will enjoy a delicious _____ tomorrow.

3. We are honoring a girl who became a _____.

4. She saved a puppy that was too _____ to swim.

5. A reporter wrote a story about the girl and made her

   _____.

6. The musicians marched behind the band _____.

7. My _____ arms got burned from too much sun.

8. I had to _____ for my mother in the crowd.

9. Mom was _____ as she put lotion on my skin.

10. This is the best party ever! Don't you _____?

Words in Context

Read the biography about Dr. Martin Luther King, Jr.
Then write a sentence to answer each question below.

> ## Dr. Martin Luther King, Jr.
>
> Dr. Martin Luther King, Jr., was a great leader. He worked hard to make life better for everyone. He helped all people, both the weak and the strong. He was a kind and gentle man.
>
> Dr. King showed people how to work together. He led peaceful marches and made speeches that excited everyone. His most famous speech is called, "I Have a Dream." He dreamed that one day all Americans would be free and live together in peace.
>
> Dr. King was born on January 15, 1929. He died in 1968. Today, people agree that Dr. King is a hero. In 1983, his birthday became a national holiday.

1. Why was Dr. Martin Luther King, Jr., a great **leader**? _____

_____

2. What was Dr. King like as a person? _____

_____

3. What is the name of Dr. King's **famous** speech? _____

_____

4. Why is Dr. King a **hero** to many people? _____

_____

Write Your Own

> bare   feast   notice   search

5. Write a sentence using a word in the box. _____

_____

Word Games

Find the word in the box that matches the clue.
Write the word in the puzzle.

agree	bare	famous	feast	gentle
hero	leader	notice	search	weak

ACROSS

3. not strong

4. to see something

5. well-known by everyone

8. the U.S. President, for example

9. think the same way

DOWN

1. a brave person

2. not rough

5. a special meal

6. to look hard for something

7. not covered

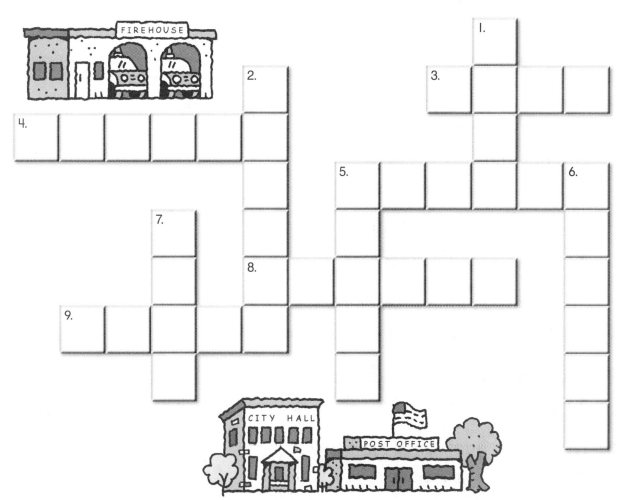

Synonyms

*Circle the word that has almost the <u>same</u> meaning as the word or words in **dark print.** Write the word on the line.*

1. The star of the show is **well-known.**

    A. weak   **B.** bright   **C.** famous   _____

2. We did not **see** that my brother was behind us.

    A. notice   **B.** search   **C.** warn   _____

3. We **look** for acorns in the forest.

    A. chew   **B.** search   **C.** warn   _____

4. The new coin is silver and **shiny.**

    A. pale   **B.** bright   **C.** famous   _____

5. The rabbit ran into the **woods.**

    A. hero   **B.** island   **C.** forest   _____

Antonyms

*Circle the word that has almost the <u>opposite</u> meaning as the word in **dark print.** Write the word on the line.*

1. The boy runs on **strong** legs.

    A. weak   **B.** famous   **C.** bare   _____

2. My brother and I **fight** about everything.

    A. chew   **B.** search   **C.** agree   _____

3. I cannot read in the **dim** light.

    A. bare   **B.** bright   **C.** pale   _____

4. The **wild** animal licked its pup.

    A. weak   **B.** gentle   **C.** pale   _____

5. We had a **snack** after the show.

    A. inn   **B.** island   **C.** feast   _____

Classifying

Look at the words in the box. Write each word in the group in which it best fits. Use each word once.

chew	hero	inn	island
leader	nibble	search	warn

Words That Tell About Eating

_____

_____

Words That Name Places

_____

_____

Words About a Special Person

_____

_____

Words That Show Action

_____

_____

Word Associations

Choose the answer that best completes the sentence or answers the question. Pay attention to the word in **dark print**. Fill in the circle next to the answer.

REVIEW UNITS 5–6

1. What things can you make with **flour**?
   - ○ trees
   - ○ cupcakes
   - ○ pictures

2. What can you do for one **hour**?
   - ○ hold my breath
   - ○ jump rope
   - ○ play at the park

3. Try to be **gentle** when you
   - ○ hold a nail and hammer.
   - ○ eat lunch.
   - ○ touch a baby.

4. When can the moon be very **bright**?
   - ○ at midnight
   - ○ at noon
   - ○ in the morning

5. What kinds of food would a rabbit **nibble**?
   - ○ fish, honey, bugs
   - ○ carrots, lettuce, celery
   - ○ soup, rice, meat

6. What would you most likely ride on to get to an **island**?
   - ○ a train
   - ○ a boat
   - ○ a bike

7. You might **warn** someone about
   - ○ walking on an icy lake.
   - ○ taking a nap.
   - ○ finding a pencil.

8. What colors are **pale**?
   - ○ red, purple, orange
   - ○ pink, gray, light blue
   - ○ yellow, black, green

9. You might walk with **bare** feet when you are
   - ○ in the forest.
   - ○ at an inn.
   - ○ at the beach.

10. You might put up a **notice** to tell people that
    - ○ your cat is lost.
    - ○ your telephone is ringing.
    - ○ you swept the floor.

Completing the Idea

Complete each sentence starter so that it makes sense.
*Pay attention to the word in **dark print**.*

1. I **agree** with my friend when she says _____

   _____

2. George Washington is **famous** because _____

   _____

3. My favorite foods at a **feast** are _____

   _____

4. I am **gentle** when I _____

   _____

5. My favorite **hero** is _____

   _____

6. Every day, I **notice** that _____

   _____

7. I **chew** my food well because _____

   _____

8. When I go to the **forest**, I see _____

   _____

9. I am a **leader** when I _____

   _____

10. Every morning, I **search** for _____

   _____

Word Study • Homophones

A **homophone** is a word that sounds just like another word but has a different meaning and spelling.

Flower and **flour** are homophones.

The rose is my favorite **flower**.
I need a cup of **flour** to make the pie crust.

Read the words in exercises 1–5. Find a homophone in the box for each word. Write the homophone on the line next to the word.

> bare   hour   inn   pale   weak

1. pail _____   4. bear _____

2. our _____   5. week _____

3. in _____

Read each sentence. If the homophone in **dark print** is used correctly, write **yes**. If it is not, then cross it out and write the correct homophone on the line.

6. I put the water in the **pale**. _____

7. I will go to sleep in an **hour**. _____

8. My legs feel **weak** from running. _____

9. I will pick the prettiest **flour**. _____

10. The **bare** ate honey from the tree. _____

Shades of Meaning • Word Choice 1

You learned the meaning of the word **search** on page 61.
Look at the chart for words that are close in meaning to
search. Notice how the meanings of the words are alike
and different.

look	When you **look** at something, you use your eyes to see it. You use your eyes to **look** at a picture.
search	When you **search** for something, you look long and hard for it. Something you **search** for might be hard to find.
watch	When you **watch** something, you look at it for quite some time. It might take an hour to **watch** a movie.

Write the word from the chart that best completes each sentence.

1. When my dog ran away, I went to _____ for it.

2. I like to _____ my brother dance.

3. We had to _____ through the closet for my hat.

4. I like to _____ out the window when I'm in the car.

5. It's fun to _____ at pictures of faraway places.

6. We woke up early to _____ the sunrise.

*In each exercise, circle the word in **dark print** to answer the
first question. Then answer the second question. Use the word
you chose in your answer.*

7. Would you **search** or **watch** someone do a trick? Why?

_____

8. Would you **watch** or **search** for a lost shoe? Why?

_____

Match the Meaning

Choose the word that best matches the meaning.
Fill in the circle next to the word.

1. a path
   - ○ forest
   - ○ feast
   - ○ trail
   - ○ flour

2. the middle
   - ○ center
   - ○ rainbow
   - ○ branch
   - ○ stack

3. to take a trip
   - ○ dash
   - ○ search
   - ○ float
   - ○ travel

4. far down
   - ○ bright
   - ○ bare
   - ○ enormous
   - ○ deep

5. to go by
   - ○ arrive
   - ○ pass
   - ○ cross
   - ○ stack

6. a small body of water
   - ○ ocean
   - ○ stream
   - ○ beach
   - ○ bridge

7. something to sit on
   - ○ evening
   - ○ leader
   - ○ bench
   - ○ seashell

8. something you can cross by car
   - ○ wave
   - ○ ocean
   - ○ bridge
   - ○ hour

9. where you find sand and seashells
   - ○ beach
   - ○ stream
   - ○ inn
   - ○ snowstorm

10. easy to see through
    - ○ tiny
    - ○ brave
    - ○ fresh
    - ○ clear

Completing the Sentence

Choose the word that best completes the sentence.
Fill in the circle next to the word.

11. On Sunday, I can _____ sleep late.
   ○ clear   ○ finally   ○ exactly   ○ center

12. We plan to _____ at the movie on time.
   ○ float   ○ warn   ○ cross   ○ arrive

13. A large _____ waits on the ticket line.
   ○ seashell   ○ rainbow   ○ crowd   ○ island

14. There aren't many seats left, so I start to _____.
   ○ worry   ○ pass   ○ chew   ○ nibble

15. After eating all of the popcorn by myself, I feel _____.
   ○ tiny   ○ greedy   ○ pale   ○ brave

16. During the movie, I must _____ when I talk.
   ○ whisper   ○ frown   ○ wave   ○ signal

17. "Is it fun to be an actor?" I _____.
   ○ frown   ○ worry   ○ travel   ○ wonder

18. The knight who fights a dragon is _____.
   ○ fresh   ○ brave   ○ wise   ○ deep

19. Seeing two movies in one day is a great _____!
   ○ bench   ○ signal   ○ idea   ○ crowd

20. I will go to the movies again next _____.
   ○ weekend   ○ hero   ○ midnight   ○ snowstorm

Vocabulary for Comprehension

Read the passage about an amazing gorilla. Then answer the questions on page 75.

Koko and Penny Patterson with a pet cat

Koko the Gorilla

Koko is a **famous** gorilla. She can use her hands to make signs for words. In this way, she "talks" to people.

Koko was born in a zoo. When she was a baby, she became **weak** and sickly. After special care, Koko became healthy. Soon she met Penny Patterson. Penny became her teacher. She started teaching Koko simple signs for words like *eat* and *drink*. Koko now knows over one thousand signs.

When Koko was fifteen years old, Penny gave her a **present**. Penny let Koko choose a pet. Koko picked out a **tiny** gray kitten that had no tail. She named him "Smoky." Koko was **gentle** with Smoky. She treated him like a baby.

No one is sure exactly how much Koko knows, but most people can **agree** that Koko is one smart gorilla.

Choose the answer that best completes the sentence or answers the question. Fill in the circle next to the answer.

21. The word **famous** means
    ○ sad.
    ○ well known.
    ○ very tired.

22. What special skill does Koko have?
    ○ She can talk to cats.
    ○ She can use hand signs.
    ○ She can speak words.

23. What does the word **weak** mean?
    ○ not warm
    ○ heavy
    ○ not strong

24. In this passage, the word **present** means
    ○ here.
    ○ show.
    ○ gift.

25. What does the word **tiny** mean?
    ○ very large
    ○ very small
    ○ striped

26. What does the word **gentle** mean?
    ○ soft and mild
    ○ angry and loud
    ○ shy and scared

27. What word can you use to describe Koko?
    ○ mean
    ○ small
    ○ smart

28. What would make another good title for this passage?
    ○ "Smoky the Kitten"
    ○ "A Gorilla That Can Sign"
    ○ "All About Gorillas"

29. When people **agree**, they
    ○ think the same way.
    ○ get into a fight.
    ○ do not like each other.

30. The author most likely wrote this passage to
    ○ tell a story about a kitten.
    ○ give facts about a real gorilla.
    ○ teach people sign language.

Introducing the Words

Listen to this article about the amazing world of insects. Pay attention to the words in the color boxes. These are the words you will be learning in this unit.

Be an Outdoor Detective

(Magazine Article)

In the animal world around us, there are lots of small creatures waiting for you to discover. Many of these critters belong to the insect family. All insects have three main body parts and six legs. However, insects come in all shapes, sizes, and colors. They can be found anywhere from a dry desert to a damp swamp.

Some insects are so small that you may need a tool such as a hand lens to see them. Other insects have features that make

them easy to find. For example, you can easily see a colorful butterfly on a plant. And, you will know it when a bee is buzzing like an alarm near your ear.

Many insects are quite busy at work. When butterflies and bees land on flowers, their bodies often pick up a powder called pollen. Then when they fly to other flowers, they scatter the pollen. This helps create more plants.

Sometimes, insects work as a team. Ants are a good example. Ants work in groups called colonies. A single colony may have hundreds or even thousands of ants in it. Together, the ants work to build anthills and tunnels in soil or sand. These places give the ants a place to stay safe. Ants also work together to collect pieces of plants or food crumbs that people leave behind. Then the ants carry this food back to the anthill. Ants can even carry pieces of food that are bigger than their bodies!

Are you ready to start exploring? Pay attention to where you step, and look closely at leaves and dirt. You may see some interesting insects.

Word Meanings

You heard the words below in the passage on pages 76–77.
Read each word and its meaning. Write the word on the
line to complete the sentence.

1. alarm
(noun)

An **alarm** is something that wakes people or warns
them of danger. It could be a bell or a buzzer.

When the kitchen got smoky, an

_____ sounded.

2. collect
(verb)

When you gather things together, you **collect** them.

I like to _____ seashells at the shore.

3. damp
(adjective)

When something is **damp**, it is a little wet or moist.

My shoes got wet in the rain and are

still _____.

4. insect
(noun)

An **insect** is a small animal with three main
body parts, six legs, wings, and no backbone.
Bees, flies, and moths are **insects**.

A dragonfly is an _____
found near fresh water.

5. plant
(noun)

A **plant** is a living thing that grows in soil or in
water. It often has green leaves.

A tree is a kind of _____.

(verb)

You **plant** when you put something such as a
seed into the ground so it can grow.

When is the best time to _____ tulips?

6. safe
(adjective)

If something is **safe**, it is not in danger of being harmed or stolen.

Always put on a seatbelt to be

_____ in a car.

(noun)

A **safe** is a strong box in which you can lock up money and other valuable things.

Holly keeps her special rings

in a _____.

---

7. scatter
(verb)

When you **scatter** things, you throw them over a large area.

The children like to _____ bread crumbs in the pond for the ducks.

---

8. soil
(noun)

Soil is the dirt or earth that plants grow in.

Plants need light, water, air, and

_____ to grow.

---

9. team
(noun)

A **team** is a group of people who work together or play a sport together.

There are eleven players on a soccer

_____.

---

10. tool
(noun)

A **tool** is a piece of equipment used to do a certain job.

*A hammer is a _____
we use to pound nails.*

Match the Meaning

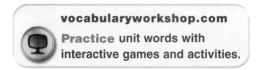
*Choose the word from the box that matches the meaning
in the clue. Write the word on the line.*

| alarm | collect | damp | plant | scatter |

1. You do this when you put seeds into the ground.

_____

2. You do this when you save stamps or coins. _____

3. You feel this way when you are in a light rain. _____

4. You hear this during a fire drill. _____

5. You do this to leaves when you throw them in the air.

_____

| insect | safe | soil | team | tool |

6. This is often needed to fix something. _____

7. This is a place to keep money. _____

8. This is the dirt a plant grows in. _____

9. This group of people works together. _____

10. This small creature has wings and six legs. _____

Completing the Sentence

Choose the word from the box that best completes the sentence. Write the word on the line.

alarm	collect	damp	insect	plant
safe	scatter	soil	team	tool

1. Jess wakes up as soon as the _____ goes off.

2. Today her softball _____ has a big job to do!

3. First, the children _____ things for gardening.

4. Then they search the ground for fresh _____.

5. They use a _____ for digging deep.

6. After that, they _____ seeds.

7. Finally, the children water the soil so it is _____.

8. They want to keep out any bird or _____.

9. They worry that the seeds will not be _____.

10. Soon each seed will grow into a _____!

Words in Context

Read the directions on the card. Then write a sentence to answer each question below.

How to Grow an Avocado Plant

Here's a plant that is easy to grow. You don't even need soil or a tool to dig with!

a. First collect the following things:
- an avocado pit • a jar • four toothpicks • water

b. Stick in the toothpicks around the center of the pit. To be safe, don't touch the sharp ends of the toothpicks.

c. Fill the jar part-way with water.

d. Place the bigger end of the pit in the water so the toothpicks rest on the top of the jar.

e. Finally, place the jar in a bright window.

Don't forget to clean up with a damp cloth!

1. What do these directions tell you? _____

_____

2. What things do you have to **collect**? _____

_____

3. How might toothpicks not be **safe**? _____

_____

4. Which word on the card means "moist" or "a little wet"? _____

_____

Write Your Own

| alarm | insect | scatter | team |

5. Write a sentence using a word in the box. _____

_____

Word Games

Find the word in the box that matches the clue.
Write each letter of the word on an answer blank.

alarm	collect	damp	insect	plant
safe	scatter	soil	team	tool

1. a hammer or a saw   __ __ __ __

2. not full of danger   __ __ __ __

3. to throw all over   __ __ __ __ __ __ __

4. to gather   __ __ __ __ __ __ __

5. dirt to plant in   __ __ __ __

6. it grows in water or soil   __ __ __ __ __

7. a little wet   __ __ __ __

8. a group that plays sports   __ __ __ __

9. a loud warning sound   __ __ __ __ __

10. what a housefly is   __ __ __ __ __ __

Look at the letters you wrote in the shaded column above.
Write them on the answer blanks below to answer the riddle.

What do you call two bananas?

A pair __ __   __ __ __ __ __ __ __

Introducing the Words

Listen to this article about beautiful Yellowstone National Park. Pay attention to the words in the color boxes. These are the words you will be learning in this unit.

Yellowstone National Park

(Magazine Article)

Yellowstone National Park is our country's first national park. It is a large park. Parts of it are in three states: Wyoming, Montana, and Idaho. The park is famous for its natural wonders, such as waterfalls, hot springs, and geysers.

There are many reasons to visit Yellowstone National Park. One is to see the many geysers. A geyser is a natural hot spring that sprays steam and hot water into the air. The most famous geyser is Old Faithful. It can prove to you that it deserves its name. About every ninety minutes, Old Faithful blasts a steady stream of boiling water high into the sky.

A geyser sprays steam and hot water into the air.

Another reason to visit the park is to see hot springs and thick mud pots. The mud pots are pools of hot muddy water. Don't dive in though! Some are as hot as boiling water.

Yellowstone is home to many animals. You may be able to get a close look at a herd of wild bison, sometimes called buffalo, from your car. Many years ago, hunters were an enemy of the bison. Now the bison in the park are protected. Elk, moose, bears, and wolves are among the other animals that live in

A bison mother and calf graze in the park.

Yellowstone. Eagles, too, soar through its skies. Visitors should remember not to bother, feed, or frighten the animals in the park.

People can walk on the park's many miles of smooth walking trails. People can also camp, boat, and horseback ride. Visitors should pack a map, water, and camera. It is a good idea to seal the camera in a plastic bag to protect it from water.

Yellowstone has many amazing things to see. No wonder over sixty million people have visited this special place!

YELLOWSTONE NATIONAL PARK

NATIONAL PARK SERVICE

Department of the Interior

Word Meanings

You heard the words below in the passage on pages 84–85.
Read each word and its meaning. Write the word on the
line to complete the sentence.

1. **dive**
(verb)

When you **dive**, you go head first into
water with your arms stretched out in
front of you.

*Rick knows to _____
into the deep end of the pool.*

2. **enemy**
(noun)

An **enemy** is a person or animal that doesn't like,
or wants to harm, another person or animal.

A hunter is an animal's _____.

3. **frighten**
(verb)

When you **frighten** someone, you scare the person.

*Yoko can _____ her brother by
wearing a scary mask.*

4. **herd**
(noun)

A **herd** is a group of animals. The
herd may feed or travel together.

*A _____ of
cattle wanders in the meadow.*

5. **pack**
(verb)

When you **pack**, you put things into a container,
such as a bag, box, or suitcase.

I will _____ my books for school.

(noun)

A **pack** is a group of something, such as animals,
people, or things.

There are six crayons in a _____.

6. prove
(verb)

When you **prove** something, you show that it is true.

The experiment will _____ that plants need sun to grow.

---

7. seal
(noun)

A **seal** is a sea animal that has thick fur and flippers. It can swim and live in cold places.

The _____ uses its flippers to pull itself along the ground.

(verb)

When you **seal** something, you close it up tightly.

Use tape to _____ the box before you mail it.

---

8. smooth
(adjective)

If something is **smooth**, it is flat and even, not rough and bumpy.

A baby's skin is soft and _____.

---

9. soar
(verb)

To **soar** is to fly very high in the air.

Watch the bald eagle

_____ in the sky.

---

10. steady
(adjective)

If something is **steady**, it continues and does not change much.

We played inside all day because of the

_____ rainfall.

Match the Meaning

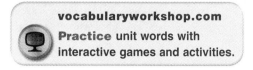
Choose the word from the box that matches the meaning in the clue. Write the word on the line.

dive	frighten	pack	prove	seal

1. You might use a pool to do this. _____

2. You use tape or glue to do this to a box. _____

3. You do this to convince someone that something is true.

_____

4. You do this when you scare someone. _____

5. You do this when you put clothes in a suitcase. _____

enemy	herd	smooth	soar	steady

6. This is what a plane can do. _____

7. This is a group of horses. _____

8. This is what a spider is to a fly. _____

9. This is how a frozen lake looks. _____

10. A tightrope walker needs to be sure he feels this when he works.

_____

Completing the Sentence

Choose the word from the box that best completes the
sentence. Write the word on the line.

dive	enemy	frighten	herd	pack
prove	seal	smooth	soar	steady

1. Jack is ready to _____ his book bag for school.

2. He wants to _____ to his mom that he knows a lot
about animals.

3. One animal that swims in the ocean is a _____.

4. A penguin has a _____ black and white body.

5. Dolphins jump and _____ into the sea.

6. Zebras live in a _____ to stay safe.

7. A turtle's shell keeps it safe from its _____.

8. A bear may climb a tree when people _____ it.

9. Mom wonders how a lion is _____ on a tree limb.

10. Jack wonders what it is like to _____ like a bird.

Words in Context

Read the article about elephants. Then write a sentence to answer each question below.

Enormous Elephants

The elephant is the biggest living land animal. Its thick skin is wrinkled, not smooth. Twenty to forty elephants live in a herd of family members. During the day, the herd stands in the shade and sleeps.

In the evening, elephants look for food. They walk slowly so the young and old can keep up. At a stream they drink and wash. They swim in deep water but can't jump or dive.

Other animals don't frighten elephants, not even a pack of wild dogs. People are their only enemy. Don't try to prove this! You wouldn't want an enormous, six-ton elephant running after you!

1. How would you describe the skin of an elephant? _____

_____

2. How would you describe a **herd** of elephants? _____

_____

3. What two words in the article are other words for "group"? _____

_____

4. Why do you think other animals don't **frighten** elephants? _____

_____

Write Your Own

> seal   soar   steady

5. Write a sentence using a word in the box. _____

_____

Word Games

Find the word in the box that matches the clue.
Write the word on the line.

| dive | enemy | frighten | herd | pack |
| prove | seal | smooth | soar | steady |

1. not bumpy _____

2. not a friend _____

3. to put things in a box _____

4. to fly up high _____

5. to scare _____

6. to go in head first _____

7. not shaking _____

8. an animal with thick fur and flippers _____

9. to show that something is true _____

10. like a pack _____

**Look at the words you wrote. Find
them in the puzzle and circle them.**

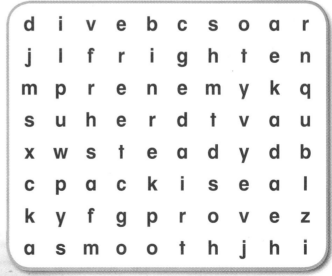

d	i	v	e	b	c	s	o	a	r
j	l	f	r	i	g	h	t	e	n
m	p	r	e	n	e	m	y	k	q
s	u	h	e	r	d	t	v	a	u
x	w	s	t	e	a	d	y	d	b
c	p	a	c	k	i	s	e	a	l
k	y	f	g	p	r	o	v	e	z
a	s	m	o	o	t	h	j	h	i

Synonyms

*Circle the word that has almost the <u>same</u> meaning as the word in **dark print**. Write the word on the line.*

1. A beetle is a kind of **bug.**
   A. plant   **B.** tool   **C.** insect   _____

2. A loud noise might **scare** you.
   A. frighten   **B.** scatter   **C.** soar   _____

3. A **group** of lions will frighten the deer.
   A. seal   **B.** pack   **C.** enemy   _____

4. How can you **show** that this statement is true?
   A. pack   **B.** scatter   **C.** prove   _____

5. We heard the **even** beat of the drum.
   A. safe   **B.** steady   **C.** damp   _____

Antonyms

*Circle the word that has almost the <u>opposite</u> meaning as the word in **dark print**. Write the word on the line.*

1. Can you help me **open** the box?
   A. plant   **B.** seal   **C.** collect   _____

2. Please **collect** the birdseed in the cage.
   A. soar   **B.** plant   **C.** scatter   _____

3. An ant's **friend** may be another ant.
   A. alarm   **B.** enemy   **C.** team   _____

4. The boy skated across the **bumpy** ice.
   A. safe   **B.** damp   **C.** smooth   _____

5. The sand of the beach was **dry**.
   A. damp   **B.** safe   **C.** steady   _____

REVIEW UNITS 7–8

Classifying

Look at the words in the box. Write each word in the group in which it best fits. Use each word once.

> dive   herd   insect   plant
> seal   soar   soil   team

Garden Words

_____

_____

Action Words

_____

_____

Words That Name Groups

_____

_____

Words That Name Creatures

_____

_____

Word Associations

*Choose the answer that best completes the sentence or answers the question. Pay attention to the word in **dark print**. Fill in the circle next to the answer.*

1. A **tool** used to cut wood is a
   - ○ knife.
   - ○ saw.
   - ○ hammer.

2. What might you **collect** to recycle?
   - ○ old newspapers
   - ○ teams
   - ○ milk

3. A towel feels **damp** when you
   - ○ buy it from the store.
   - ○ use it to dry your hands.
   - ○ take it out of the closet.

4. Where might you find a lot of **soil**?
   - ○ in the air
   - ○ in the ground
   - ○ in the ocean

5. What does an **alarm** tell a firefighter to do?
   - ○ get on the fire truck
   - ○ eat lunch
   - ○ drink water

6. A cat is an **enemy** of a
   - ○ mouse.
   - ○ whale.
   - ○ seal.

7. Where might you see a **pack** of wolves?
   - ○ in a card shop
   - ○ in a box
   - ○ in a wooded area

8. What might **frighten** you?
   - ○ a sleeping baby
   - ○ a new friend
   - ○ a door slamming shut

9. It is **safe** to cross the street after you
   - ○ dash across it.
   - ○ see the signal turn red.
   - ○ look both ways.

10. What is something you might **scatter**?
    - ○ bread crumbs
    - ○ snowballs
    - ○ fish

Completing the Idea

Complete each sentence starter so that it makes sense.
*Pay attention to the word in **dark print**.*

1. When my **alarm** goes off each morning, _____

_____

2. When I go away, I **pack** _____

_____

3. A **team** of people _____

_____

4. When I **dive** into the pool, I _____

_____

5. I watch the birds **soar** over _____

_____

6. If the ice on the pond is **smooth,** _____

_____

7. My gloves are **damp** because _____

_____

8. I can **prove** that _____

_____

9. I like to **collect** _____

_____

10. A **tool** that Dad uses in the garden is _____

_____

Word Study • Prefixes

A **prefix** is a word part that is added to the beginning of a word. A prefix changes the meaning of the word.

The prefix **un** can mean "not."

un + clear = unclear

Unclear means "not clear."

The prefix **re** can mean "again."

re + stack = restack

Restack means "to stack again."

*Write the prefix **un** or **re** to make a word that goes with the meaning shown. Then write the whole word.*

1. not safe = _____safe _____

2. seal again = _____seal _____

3. not steady = _____steady _____

4. pack again = _____pack _____

5. plant again = _____plant _____

*Complete each sentence with a word from the box. Add **un** or **re** to the word so that the word makes sense in the sentence.*

| pack | plant | safe | seal | steady |

6. I was _____ riding my bike on the rocky trail.

7. I will have to _____ the lunch bag if I put in more food.

8. To send back the books, you must _____ the box.

9. Since no flowers grew, we will _____ the seeds.

10. It is _____ to run in the street.

Shades of Meaning • Analogies 2

You learned two ways in which words can go together.

large / big
> **Think**
> **Large** and **big** have almost the same meaning.

hot / cold ➤
> **Think**
> **Hot** and **cold** have opposite meanings.

Here is another way words can go together.

apple / fruit
> **Think**
> An **apple** is a kind of **fruit**.

dog / animal
> **Think**
> A **dog** is a kind of **animal**.

Read each pair of words. Write a sentence that tells how the words go together.

1. butterfly / insect _____

2. rake / tool _____

3. steady / shaky _____

4. cactus / plant _____

5. gather / collect _____

6. enemy / friend _____

7. soar / fly _____

8. bench / seat _____

9. search / hunt _____

UNIT 9

Introducing the Words

Listen to this passage about a boy's experience at a school field day. Pay attention to the words in the color boxes. These are the words you will be learning in this unit.

Field Day!
(Personal Narrative)

I love to play sports at any time of the year. I'll even shiver through a soccer game in November. My favorite sports day of all is Field Day. It takes place during the last week of school. Everyone in school is on one of four teams. I am on the Blue Team.

Our teachers set up all the games before we get to school. They must wake up at dawn! They also make sure everyone is fair and plays by the rules. Yesterday, my favorite day was finally here. I couldn't wait to play and cheer for my team!

The first event of the day was an obstacle course. We had to hop through tires, run around cones, and crawl through a tube. I ran into trouble early. My foot got stuck in one of the tires. I tripped and let out a loud cry of pain. Luckily, the fall didn't do much harm. I just scraped my elbow.

Soon I was ready for the next event, the potato race. Each set of partners was given a potato on a spoon to carry back and forth across a long field of grass. To win, the partners had to go the entire way without dropping the potato. Each person had to stay calm and walk carefully. It's easy for the potato to fall off of the spoon. During my turn, I could see the potato tremble on the spoon, but it didn't drop. When I reached the finish line, I saw my partner jumping up and down. We had won the race! Our win put our team in first place. I felt like a hero!

Word Meanings

You heard the words below in the passage on pages 98–99.
Read each word and its meaning. Write the word on the
line to complete the sentence.

1. **calm**
   (adjective)

   If something is **calm**, it is quiet and still.

   The ducks swam on the

   _____ lake.

2. **cheer**
   (verb)

   When people **cheer**, they yell or call out loudly.

   *The fans _____ for the
   home team.*

3. **dawn**
   (noun)

   Dawn is the time of day when the sun
   first comes up.

   Some people wake up at _____.

4. **entire**
   (adjective)

   Entire means the whole thing. It is all of something.

   We were so thirsty that we drank the

   _____ jug of water.

5. **fair**
   (adjective)

   A person who is **fair** follows the rules and treats
   everyone the same way.

   Ed was _____ and gave me a turn.

   (noun)

   A **fair** is an outdoor place where
   people bring things to sell. It is
   a place where people have fun.

   I had fun on the rides at

   the _____.

6. field
(noun)

A **field** is an area where a game is played. Usually, a field is covered with grass.

The boy ran onto the _____ to join his teammates.

(noun)

A **field** is a large open area that has no trees. Sometimes, a field is used to grow things.

The horses ate the grass in

the _____.

7. harm
(verb)

Harm means "to hurt."

I stepped over the frog so that I would not

_____ it.

8. pain
(noun)

A **pain** is a feeling of hurt.

I felt _____ in my arm after I fell.

9. shiver
(verb)

When you **shiver**, you shake quickly. Usually, your whole body will shiver if you are cold or afraid.

The cold, blowing wind made me

_____.

10. tremble
(verb)

When you **tremble**, you shake from excitement or anger. A part of your body shakes a little when you tremble.

My fingers _____ before I play the piano for my teacher.

Match the Meaning

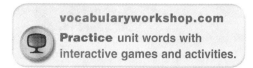
Choose the word from the box that matches the meaning in the clue. Write the word on the line.

> calm   cheer   entire   pain   shiver

I. You feel this when you are hurt. _____

2. You use this word to tell about the whole thing.

_____

3. You do this when you call out loudly for your team.

_____

4. You feel this way when you are not upset. _____

5. You do this when you feel cold. _____

> dawn   fair   field   harm   tremble

6. This is a grassy place where games are played.

_____

7. This is what your lips might do when you feel afraid.

_____

8. This is what loud noise can do to your ears. _____

9. This is the beginning of the day. _____

10. This is where you might play games and eat apple pie.

_____

Completing the Sentence

Choose the word from the box that best completes the
sentence. Write the word on the line.

calm	cheer	dawn	entire	fair
field	harm	pain	shiver	tremble

1. I woke up at _____ on the big day.

2. It was the day of the school _____.

3. I ran downstairs and felt a _____ in my foot.

4. I tripped over a toy, but I did not _____ my foot.

5. I passed the _____ on my way to school.

6. The _____ class was waiting for me.

7. I was so cold that I began to _____ all over.

8. The race began and I felt very _____.

9. I dashed to the finish line and everyone began to

   _____.

10. I was so happy that my lips began to _____.

Words in Context

Read the story. Then write a sentence to answer each question below.

Jets Win Big!

The entire town seemed to be at Williams Field last Friday. Why? To see if the Bears could beat the Jets one more time. It's been a bad year for the Jets. It lost Erin Nelson in the first game. She fell and had a bad pain in her arm.

On Friday, the Jets remained calm before the game. It didn't take long to find out why. Erin Nelson ran out onto the field, followed by her team. Erin and the team scored goal after goal. The Bears could hear the crowd cheer. Then the game was over, and the score was 10–0. The Jets won fair and square!

1. Where and when was the game played? _____

_____

2. Why was nearly the **entire** town at the game? _____

_____

3. Why do you think the Jets felt **calm** the day of the game? _____

_____

4. Why did the crowd **cheer**? _____

_____

Write Your Own

| dawn | harm | shiver | tremble |

5. Write a sentence using a word in the box. _____

_____

Word Games

Find the word in the box that matches the clue.
Write the word in the puzzle.

calm	cheer	dawn	entire	fair
field	harm	pain	shiver	tremble

ACROSS

3. shout or yell

5. not just a part

7. not angry or upset

8. where grass can grow

9. to shake in the cold

DOWN

1. what a mouse did when caught

2. what you get with a headache

4. to hurt or cause pain

6. when the sun rises

8. not cheating

Introducing the Words

Listen to this biography about two brothers who invented and flew the first engine-driven plane. Pay attention to the words in the color boxes. These are the words you will be learning in this unit.

The Wright Brothers

(Biography)

It is hard to believe that the first airplane with an engine flew just over 100 years ago. The hard work and clever thinking of Wilbur and Orville Wright made it happen.

The Wright brothers took an early interest in flying. As children, they had a toy helicopter that made them curious about flight. When the helicopter broke, the boys built their own model. That showed them not to doubt their skill at making things. As adults, the brothers built bicycles, printing presses, and kites. They also liked to make gliders, which are planes without engines.

Listen to this passage at vocabularyworkshop.com.

In the 1890s, flying in gliders was dangerous. The Wright brothers were eager to make flying safer. They thought that an engine would give pilots more control.

In 1900, Orville and Wilbur went to the windy village of Kitty Hawk, North Carolina. There, they kept testing new airplane designs. Three years later, they had a model that worked. The plane was 16 feet wide and made of wood and cloth. It had a gas engine.

The first flight took off on December 17, 1903. Orville would board the plane and squeeze tightly to hold on and control the plane. The engine would start with a screech. The plane flew in the air for 120 feet. The trip lasted 12 seconds and ended with a mild crash. There was some fear that the plane was damaged, but Wilbur flew it again a few hours later. You would have to leap for joy at the sight if you had been there.

In 1905, the Wright brothers built an airplane that could fly for 30 minutes. On December 31, 1908, Wilbur flew a plane for a record-breaking 2 hours and 19 minutes. The Wright brothers kept working to build better airplanes.

Word Meanings

You heard the words below in the passage on pages 106–107.
Read each word and its meaning. Write the word on the line
to complete the sentence.

1. board
  (noun)

A **board** is a long, flat piece of wood or plastic.

The man used the _____
to finish building the doghouse.

  (verb)

If you **board** a bus, you get on it.
You might also board a train or boat.

The women will _____ the train
with their bags.

2. curious
  (adjective)

If you are **curious**, you want to
learn or find out about something.

The kitten is _____
about the new goldfish.

3. dangerous
  (adjective)

Something that is **dangerous** is not safe.
It could cause harm.

Riding a bike without a helmet can be

_____.

4. doubt
  (verb)

If you **doubt** something, you are not sure about it.

I _____ that their team will
win today.

5. eager
  (adjective)

A person who is **eager** is very interested in
doing something.

The girl is _____ to play the piano.

6. fear
(noun)

Fear is a feeling that danger is near or that something bad will happen.

I feel _____ when I am in a dark place.

(verb)

If you **fear** something, you are afraid of it.

Singing in front of people is what I

_____ most.

7. leap
(noun)

If you **leap**, you take a jump forward.

Watch the frog _____ from one rock onto the other.

8. screech
(noun)

A **screech** is a loud, high sound.

The bird made a loud _____ when people came into the pet store.

(verb)

When things **screech**, they make a loud sound.

The tires _____ when I brake.

9. squeeze
(verb)

If you **squeeze** something, you hold it tightly.

The towel will dry more quickly if you

_____ the water out of it first.

10. village
(noun)

A **village** is a small town.

My grandparents live in a

small _____.

Match the Meaning

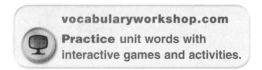
Choose the word from the box that matches the meaning in the clue. Write the word on the line.

| board   doubt   leap   screech   squeeze |

1. You do this when you hold something tightly. _____

2. You do this when you jump forward. _____

3. You do this when you get on a train. _____

4. You do this when you are not sure about something.

   _____

5. You do this when you make a high, loud noise. _____

| curious   dangerous   eager   fear   village |

6. This is what you feel when you are scared. _____

7. This word describes something that is not safe. _____

8. This word describes a person who wants to learn about something.

   _____

9. This is a small town where people live. _____

10. This word describes a person who really wants to do

    something. _____

Completing the Sentence

*Choose the word from the box that best completes the
sentence. Write the word on the line.*

board	curious	dangerous	doubt	eager
fear	leap	screech	squeeze	village

1. I have always been _____ about the fish in the sea.

2. We went to a beach near a small _____.

3. A boy was paddling in the water on a long _____.

4. I was _____ to try it, too!

5. The boy said that it was not _____ at all.

6. He told me to _____ the sides with my hands.

7. Once I got into the water, I had no _____.

8. I saw a fish _____ out of the water.

9. I fell in the cold water and heard myself _____.

10. I do not _____ that I can learn to do it!

Words in Context

Read the letter. Then write a sentence to answer each question below.

June 24

Dear Maria,

    I took my first airplane ride, and it was great fun! The first thing we did was board the plane. I was curious about what the plane was like. A woman took me into the cockpit!

    Pretty soon, the plane took off. Everything looked small from the air. I saw a village and lots of trees. When we landed, I heard a loud screech. It was the brakes! Believe me, flying is not dangerous. I am eager to do it again. Next year, I will fly to your house. Isn't that cool?

Love,
Amelia

1. What was Amelia **curious** about? _____

_____

2. Why do you think the **village** looked small from the air? _____

_____

3. What made the loud **screech** when the airplane landed? _____

_____

4. Why do you think Amelia is **eager** to fly again? _____

_____

Write Your Own

| doubt | fear | leap | squeeze |

5. Write a sentence using a word in the box. _____

_____

Word Games

Find the word in the box that matches the clue.
Write each letter of the word on an answer blank.

board	curious	dangerous	doubt	eager
fear	leap	screech	squeeze	village

1. not sure ___ ___ ___ ___ ___

2. be afraid ___ ___ ___ ___

3. small town ___ ___ ___ ___ ___ ___ ___

4. get on a plane ___ ___ ___ ___ ___

5. not a whisper ___ ___ ___ ___ ___ ___ ___

6. excited about ___ ___ ___ ___ ___

7. not safe ___ ___ ___ ___ ___ ___ ___ ___ ___

8. to spring forward ___ ___ ___ ___

9. hold tightly ___ ___ ___ ___ ___ ___ ___

10. want to know ___ ___ ___ ___ ___ ___ ___

Look at the letters you wrote in the shaded column above.
Write them on the answer blanks below to answer the riddle.

What birds never get their hair cut?

___ ___ ___ ___ ___   ___ ___ ___ ___ ___ ___ ___

Synonyms

If you need help with a word, look it up in the **Glossary** at the back of this book.

*Circle the word that has almost the <u>same</u> meaning as the word in **dark print**. Write the word on the line.*

1. We **yell** when our team wins the game.
   A. squeeze   **B.** fear   **C.** cheer   _____

2. Don't **hurt** the kittens when you pick them up.
   A. leap   **B.** harm   **C.** tremble   _____

3. The horses are in the **meadow**.
   A. field   **B.** dawn   **C.** screech   _____

4. I ate the **whole** cake.
   A. fair   **B.** curious   **C.** entire   _____

5. We had fun at the **festival**.
   A. dawn   **B.** fair   **C.** board   _____

Antonyms

*Circle the word that has almost the <u>opposite</u> meaning as the word in **dark print**. Write the word on the line.*

1. I took a walk at **sunset.**
   A. village   **B.** field   **C.** dawn   _____

2. I **know** I will pass the test.
   A. shiver   **B.** doubt   **C.** fear   _____

3. The car is **safe** to drive.
   A. dangerous   **B.** fair   **C.** eager   _____

4. I am **nervous** when I meet my new teacher.
   A. fair   **B.** entire   **C.** calm   _____

5. I **walk** over the puddle.
   A. squeeze   **B.** doubt   **C.** leap   _____

Classifying

Look at the words in the box. Write each word in the group in which it best fits. Use each word once.

cheer	curious	eager	field
screech	shiver	squeeze	village

Words That Tell How You Feel

_____

_____

Words That Name Places

_____

_____

Sound Words

_____

_____

Action Words

_____

_____

Word Associations

*Choose the answer that best completes the sentence or answers the question. Pay attention to the word in **dark print**. Fill in the circle next to the answer.*

1. You might **tremble** when you
   - ○ find your socks.
   - ○ see a big dog barking.
   - ○ play with a friend.

2. A **village** must have
   - ○ a large shopping mall.
   - ○ a few stores.
   - ○ many restaurants.

3. A cat might show **fear** by
   - ○ purring.
   - ○ eating.
   - ○ hissing.

4. You might feel **pain** in your arm if you
   - ○ eat too much food.
   - ○ throw a ball too many times.
   - ○ kick with your foot.

5. What might you do after you **board** a bus?
   - ○ find a seat
   - ○ run a race
   - ○ wait for a train

6. What might you hear at **dawn**?
   - ○ a rooster crowing
   - ○ a crowd cheering
   - ○ a school bell ringing

7. What would make you **shiver**?
   - ○ lying on a beach
   - ○ eating a sandwich
   - ○ swimming in a cold ocean

8. It woud be hard to **squeeze** a
   - ○ sponge.
   - ○ tree.
   - ○ pillow.

9. Which of these animals **screech**?
   - ○ kittens and puppies
   - ○ crows and monkeys
   - ○ whales and sharks

10. What statement would you **doubt** is true?
    - ○ Horses eat grass.
    - ○ Bears live in Alaska.
    - ○ Cows fly to the moon.

Completing the Idea

Complete each sentence starter so that it makes sense.
Pay attention to the word in dark print.

1. When I am **calm**, I _____

   _____

2. After I read the **entire** book, I _____

   _____

3. The coach was **fair** when _____

   _____

4. I **tremble** when I _____

   _____

5. I am **curious** about _____

   _____

6. The road is **dangerous** because _____

   _____

7. I **leap** when I _____

   _____

8. I use a wooden **board** to _____

   _____

9. In the farmer's **field**, I see _____

   _____

10. I am always **eager** to _____

   _____

Word Study • Suffixes

A **suffix** is a word part that is added to the end of a word.
A suffix can change the meaning of the word.

The suffix **ful** means "full of."

hope + ful = hopeful

Hopeful means "full of hope."

I am **hopeful** that we will win the game.

The suffix **less** means "without."

hope + less = hopeless

Hopeless means "without hope."

I felt **hopeless** when we were losing.

*Add the suffixes **ful** and **less** to each word below.*

1. harm _____ _____

2. pain _____ _____

3. doubt _____ _____

4. fear _____ _____

*Add **ful** or **less** to the word in **dark print** to complete the sentence.*
Be sure the word makes sense in the sentence. Write the new word
on the line.

5. The _____ dog jumped into the cold water and swam after the ball. **(fear)**

6. Brushing your teeth is easy and _____. **(pain)**

7. Eating poorly is _____ to your health. **(harm)**

8. We wanted it to snow, but we were _____ that it would. **(doubt)**

9. A bee is _____ if you leave it alone. **(harm)**

10. A bee sting can be _____. **(pain)**

Shades of Meaning • Word Choice 2

You learned the meaning of the word **leap** on page 109.
Look at the chart for words that are close in meaning to **leap**.
Notice how the meanings of the words are alike and different.

hop	When you **hop**, you use one or both legs to push up or forward into the air, but you don't go very far.
jump	When you **jump**, you use your legs to push up or forward with more force than a hop.
leap	When you **leap**, you take a big, strong jump forward.

Write the word from the chart that best completes each sentence.

1. We saw a horse _____ the fence.

2. Would you like to _____ rope with me?

3. A rabbit will _____ around looking for food.

4. Some frogs can _____ more than ten feet.

5. I can't _____ on one foot for very long!

*In each exercise, circle the word in **dark print** to answer the first question. Then answer the second question. Use the word you chose in your answer.*

6. Would you **hop** or **leap** to get over a large puddle? Why?

_____

7. Would you **leap** or **hop** to move a few inches? Why?

_____

8. Would you **jump** or **hop** on a trampoline? Why?

_____

Introducing the Words

Listen to this biography about Margaret Heffernan Borland, one of the first women to lead a cattle drive. Pay attention to the words in the color boxes. These are the words you will be learning in this unit.

Margaret Heffernan Borland: Trail Blazer

(Biography)

In 1873, a brave Texas woman set out on a long and hard trip. Her name was Margaret Heffernan Borland. With her children and a small team of workers, Margaret led a herd of cattle from Victoria, Texas, to Wichita, Kansas. The herd had over a thousand cattle!

At the time, it was odd for a woman to lead a cattle drive. Margaret was one of the first women to do it. Many people at that time did not think it was proper for a woman to do such work. Margaret, however, was a strong woman. She did not care what others thought. She had a job to do.

Margaret's trip was tense. It was not easy. A few years earlier, cattle drivers had to carve a trail through low

mountains and land covered with small trees and bushes. The trail was still rough and dangerous. It was easy to get a scrape—or worse. The tender skin of a hand or arm was no match for a thorny bush. As workers and herds of cattle traveled, the harsh sun could beam down one day. The next day, heavy rains could flood the trails.

Margaret led a type of cattle called the Texas Longhorn. A Texas Longhorn steer had very good lean meat. These cattle could survive in rough places along the trail. Texas Longhorns, however, scared easily. A coyote howling from its den could cause them to run away in a sudden rush.

The Texas Longhorns were hard to control, but Margaret made it to Wichita with most of her herd. Today, she is remembered for her independence and strength.

Word Meanings

You heard the words below in the passage on pages 120–121. Read each word and its meaning. Write the word on the line to complete the sentence.

1. beam
(noun)

A **beam** is a long, strong piece of wood or metal that holds up part of a building.

After the builders put in the last

_____, they built the roof on top.

(verb)

To **beam** is to send something out.

Faraway stars _____ light to Earth.

2. carve
(verb)

When you **carve** something, you cut into it.

I can _____ a statue out of wood.

3. den
(noun)

A **den** is where some wild animals rest.

The wolf left its _____ to eat.

4. lean
(verb)

When you **lean**, you bend in a certain direction.

_____ back to watch the night sky.

(adjective)

Something that is **lean** does not have much fat on it.

The burger had _____ meat in it.

5. odd
(adjective)

If something is **odd**, it is not what you are used to.

A June snowstorm would be _____.

(adjective)

An **odd** number cannot be divided evenly by two.

Five is an _____ number.

6. proper
(adjective)

If something is **proper**, it is right or correct.

Wear _____ clothing on cold days.

---

7. scrape
(verb)

When you **scrape** something, you rub it against a rough or sharp surface.

Help me _____ the paint off the door.

(noun)

A **scrape** is a mark made by rubbing or scratching against something rough.

I fell and got a _____ on my knee.

---

8. steer
(verb)

When you **steer** something, you move it in a certain direction.

I tried to _____ my bike in a straight line.

(noun)

A **steer** is a bull that is raised for meat.

A _____ eats grass.

---

9. tender
(adjective)

When something is **tender**, it is soft and easy to cut.

Grandpa's steaks are always

_____.

---

10. tense
(adjective)

When you are **tense**, you are not relaxed.

I felt _____ when I tried out for the school play.

SCHOOL PLAY TRYOUTS TODAY

Match the Meaning

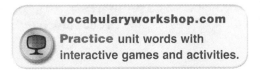
*Choose the word from the box that matches the meaning
in the clue. Write the word on the line.*

| lean | odd | scrape | tender | tense |

1. You might feel like this before a big test. _____

2. You can do this to see past someone's head in a movie theater.

   _____

3. You can cook a carrot to make it more like this. _____

4. You might do this to a table if you drag a heavy pot across the

   tabletop. _____

5. You might use this word to describe a talking cat. _____

| beam | carve | den | proper | steer |

6. This is a place where a lion sleeps at night. _____

7. This is how you make a statue out of a piece of stone.

   _____

8. This helps to hold up a skyscraper. _____

9. This is what you do to turn a car to the right or to the left.

   _____

10. This is how you might describe wearing a swimsuit to the pool.

    _____

Completing the Sentence

Choose the word from the box that best completes the sentence. Write the word on the line.

beam	carve	den	lean	odd
proper	scrape	steer	tender	tense

1. The move to our new house made us _____.

2. The number 3 in our address is an _____ number.

3. The small, nearby farm has goats and a _____.

4. One ceiling _____ had to be replaced after our move.

5. I had to _____ my head back to look at it.

6. A poster of a bear in its _____ is in my bedroom.

7. Mom had to _____ the paint off the kitchen table.

8. She had to pick the _____ tool to get the paint off.

9. Gloves protected the _____ skin on her hands.

10. This fall, we will _____ a turkey at our new table.

Words in Context

Read the article about sled dogs and sled drivers.
Then write a sentence to answer each question below.

Sled Dogs and Sled Drivers

Racing sled dogs is a big sport in some cold places. Dogs with thick fur and lean bodies are best for racing. Their lean bodies help them run quickly. Sled dogs are full of energy. Often, they are tense before a race starts.

During a race, the sled's blades carve deep lines in the snow. The driver stands in the sled to steer it. After the race, the drivers take care of their dogs. They check the tender pads on the dogs' paws. If they find a scrape, they clean it up so it will heal. Then they hand out treats for a job well done!

1. How would you describe a sled dog's body? _____

_____

2. Why might the dogs get **tense** before a race? _____

_____

3. What jobs does a sled driver have? _____

_____

4. Why might a dog get a **scrape** on its paw? _____

_____

Write Your Own

| beam | den | odd | proper |

5. Write a sentence using a word in the box. _____

_____

Word Games

Find the word in the box that matches the clue.
Write the word on the line.

beam	carve	den	lean	odd
proper	scrape	steer	tender	tense

1. how you might feel before a spelling contest _____

2. a home for a fox _____

3. wearing boots in the snow _____

4. tilt to the side _____

5. eating supper at midnight _____

6. what the sun's rays do _____

7. what you do to a piece of wood to make a boat _____

8. a perfectly cooked piece of chicken _____

9. an animal that is raised for meat _____

10. what you do when you rub mud off a shoe _____

Look at the words you wrote. Find them in the puzzle and circle them. You will find two of the words by looking down the columns.

b	f	b	e	a	m	q	w	s	p
o	q	s	c	r	a	p	e	c	t
d	v	s	t	e	e	r	a	r	o
d	s	p	e	p	r	o	p	e	r
c	a	r	v	e	a	w	e	p	d
f	k	t	e	n	s	e	m	d	e
g	e	e	r	l	e	a	n	o	n
a	g	e	p	t	e	n	d	e	r

UNIT 12

Introducing the Words

Listen to this passage about a working guide dog.
Pay attention to the words in the color boxes.
These are the words you will be learning in this unit.

A Dog with a Job

(Informational Fiction)

My name is Penny, and I work as a guide dog. The label "guide dog" means that I help a person who is blind. I was born at Guide Dogs for the Blind in San Rafael, California. This is a place that trains puppies to be guide dogs. Years ago, the company had only one dog. The modern company of today trains hundreds of dogs every year.

When I was eight weeks old, Guide Dogs for the Blind had to select a family for me. The family gave me love and a stable home. The family members taught me good manners and how to obey commands, like sit and lie down. They took me to many different places, and they played with me. Some types of play were not proper for me and were not allowed. The family members could not pitch a ball or other object for me to catch and carry back to them.

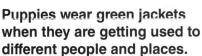

When I was eighteen months old, I went back to Guide Dogs for the Blind to begin a special training program. To be honest, I was sad to leave my family. During my training, I wore a harness. I learned how to guide a person through a busy city. I even learned fun skills like how to ride on a steep escalator. I also learned how to take a trip on a train.

Three months later, I was ready to be a guide dog. I was matched with a partner, a woman who was blind. When we met, I took a minute to sniff her hand so that I could always identify her. We trained together for three weeks. Now I have a job to do. I spend my days guiding her anywhere she wants to go. On weekends, we escape to the country, and I spend lots of time playing. I love my job.

A grown-up pup is in training at Guide Dogs for the Blind.

Puppies wear green jackets when they are getting used to different people and places.

Word Meanings

You heard the words below in the passage on pages 128–129.
Read each word and its meaning. Write the word on the line
to complete the sentence.

1. escape
(verb)

You **escape** to get away.

The dog tried to _____
through the open gate.

---

2. honest
(adjective)

If you are **honest**, you tell the truth.

I was _____ and told Dad that
I lost his pen.

---

3. label
(noun)

A **label** is a sticker or tag fastened to
something to tell more about it.

The _____ on the
can says there is enough soup
for two people.

(verb)

When you **label** something, you write
something on a sticker or tag to
tell more about it.

We should _____ all our boxes so
we know what is in each one.

---

4. modern
(adjective)

When something is **modern,** it has to do with
the present time.

In _____ times, people write
more e-mails than letters.

---

5. object
(noun)

An **object** is a thing that you can see or touch.

A ball is a round _____.

6. pitch
(verb)

When you **pitch** something, you throw it.

I tried to _____ the baseball right into the catcher's glove.

7. select
(verb)

When you **select** something, you pick it out.

At night, I _____ clothes to wear the next day.

8. sniff
(verb)

When you **sniff** something, you take in air through your nose in short, quick breaths.

My rabbit likes to _____ its food.

9. stable
(noun)

A **stable** is a building where horses are kept.

Six horses live in the _____.

(adjective)

Something that is **stable** is strong and not easily moved.

Mom fixed the chair leg to make

it more _____.

10. steep
(adjective)

A **steep** hill has a sharp slope that is difficult to go up.

We had to walk our bikes up

the _____ part of the trail.

Match the Meaning

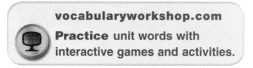
Choose the word from the box that matches the meaning in the clue. Write the word on the line.

> escape   honest   object   pitch   sniff

1. You would probably want a friend who is like this.

   _____

2. You might do this to a beautiful flower in the garden.

   _____

3. You might want to do this when you watch a boring movie.

   _____

4. You could do this with a baseball. _____

5. You might be able to hold this in your hand. _____

> label   modern   select   stable   steep

6. This kind of mountain would be hard to climb. _____

7. This might tell you what is in your cereal. _____

8. This word might describe a well-built bridge. _____

9. This word could describe a brand new car. _____

10. This is what you do when you pick the best apples from a

    big pile. _____

Completing the Sentence

Choose the word from the box that best completes the
sentence. Write the word on the line.

escape	honest	label	modern	object
pitch	select	sniff	stable	steep

1. I went to a _____ to ride a horse for the first time.

2. The _____ on the trainer's shirt said, "Sue."

3. Sue helped me _____ a horse to ride.

4. She told me to let the horse _____ my hand.

5. We closed the door so the horses would not _____.

6. Some parts of the riding path were _____.

7. If the horses saw an _____ on the path, they walked around it.

8. Horseback riding is not a _____ thing to do, but it is fun.

9. After riding, I helped _____ hay to feed the horses.

10. Riding is hard work. This is the _____ truth.

Words in Context

Read the travel brochure. Then write a
sentence to answer each question below.

Visit the Red Horse Inn

How would you like to escape to the mountains?
If you need a place to stay, look no further than the
Red Horse Inn. We're being honest when we say you'll
have a fun time here. All of our rooms are modern and
clean. If you need a toothbrush or a towel, just let us
know. We can bring you the object you need. As you
may have guessed from our name, we have a stable on
our grounds. You can go riding every day if you want!
We also have flat and steep hiking trails. Just select
what you like best!

I. What do you think it means to have **modern** rooms? _____

_____

2. Why is this place called the Red Horse Inn? _____

_____

3. What is one object the workers at the inn could bring to you?

_____

4. Which is harder to hike, a flat trail or a steep trail? _____

_____

Write Your Own

label   pitch   sniff

5. Write a sentence using a word in the box. _____

_____

Word Games

Find the word in the box that matches the clue.
Write the word in the puzzle.

escape	honest	label	modern	object
pitch	select	sniff	stable	steep

ACROSS

1. strong and not easily moved

4. what a hill might be like

8. to choose

9. not lying

DOWN

1. to take breaths through your nose

2. a tag that gives the shirt size

3. to get away

5. not old

6. something you can pick up

7. to toss

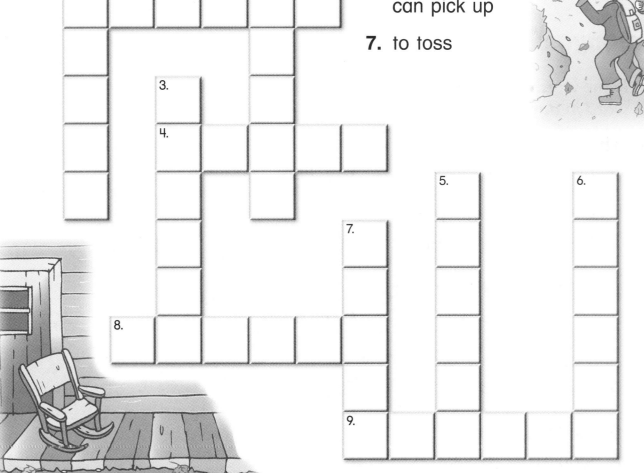

Synonyms

Circle the word that has almost the <u>same</u> meaning as the word in **dark print.** Write the word on the line.

1. It would be **strange** to have a bear as a pet.
   A. tense   **B.** honest   **C.** odd   _____

2. Can you **toss** the ball to me?
   A. beam   **B.** pitch   **C.** carve   _____

3. You can **pick** the pen you like best.
   A. scrape   **B.** select   **C.** sniff   _____

4. We saw a young **bull** at the farm.
   A. steer   **B.** label   **C.** den   _____

5. We cooked the potatoes until they were **soft**.
   A. honest   **B.** tense   **C.** tender   _____

Antonyms

Circle the word that has almost the <u>opposite</u> meaning as the word in **dark print.** Write the word on the line.

1. The road is very **flat**.
   A. proper   **B.** modern   **C.** steep   _____

2. This animal has a **fat** body.
   A. lean   **B.** stable   **C.** proper   _____

3. I felt **relaxed** at the beach.
   A. tense   **B.** steep   **C.** modern   _____

4. The house is very **old**.
   A. odd   **B.** modern   **C.** proper   _____

5. My chair is **shaky**.
   A. stable   **B.** lean   **C.** tender   _____

 # Classifying

Look at the words in the box. Write each word in the
group in which it best fits. Use each word once.

den	escape	honest	lean
pitch	proper	stable	tender

Places Where Animals Live

_____

_____

Words That Tell About Meat

_____

_____

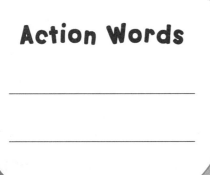
Action Words

_____

_____

Words That Tell About Your Behavior

_____

_____

REVIEW UNITS 11-12

Word Associations

*Choose the answer that best completes the sentence or answers the question. Pay attention to the word in **dark print**. Fill in the circle next to the answer.*

1. Why might you **label** your notebook?
   - ○ because it's blue
   - ○ so people know it's yours
   - ○ because you don't like it

2. What is an **odd** thing to do with your hand?
   - ○ draw a picture
   - ○ score a goal in soccer
   - ○ play piano

3. Where might you find a **beam**?
   - ○ in a house
   - ○ in a bowl of cereal
   - ○ in a baseball game

4. To make sure a pet mouse doesn't **escape**, you should
   - ○ clean out its cage.
   - ○ make sure it takes naps.
   - ○ close the door to its cage.

5. Which of these is something you **steer**?
   - ○ a farm
   - ○ an apple
   - ○ a bike

6. Which of these is a **modern** thing?
   - ○ a horse
   - ○ the Internet
   - ○ a tree

7. What might you find in a **den**?
   - ○ a baseball field
   - ○ a whale
   - ○ a sleeping wolf

8. What might cause you to **scrape** your elbow?
   - ○ falling on the sidewalk
   - ○ watching TV
   - ○ wearing a sweatshirt

9. If you feel **tense**, you
   - ○ are great at sports.
   - ○ are not calm.
   - ○ own more than nine things.

10. If a house is **stable**, it will
    - ○ stand for a long time.
    - ○ fall over.
    - ○ have to be painted red.

Completing the Idea

Complete each sentence starter so that it makes sense.
Pay attention to the word in **dark print.**

1. The **label** on the can said that _____

_____

2. When I see the sun **beam** through my window, I _____

_____

3. My favorite **object** in my room is _____

_____

4. It was **odd** to find _____

_____

5. I felt **tense** when _____

_____

6. If I **lean** my head back, I can see _____

_____

7. It is not **proper** to _____

_____

8. At the supermarket, I **select** _____

_____

9. I got a **scrape** when I _____

_____

10. I like to **sniff** _____

_____

Word Study • Dictionary: Multiple-Meaning Words

A **multiple-meaning word** is a word with more than one meaning.

> **board 1.** *(noun)* a long, flat piece of wood or plastic **2.** *(verb)* to get on a vehicle such as a ship, plane, or train

This sentence shows the second meaning (meaning 2) of **board**:

> We **board** the bus at 12 noon.

Write the word that completes each sentence. Then write 1 or 2 to show which meaning of the word is used.

> **beam 1.** *(noun)* a long, strong piece of wood or metal that holds up part of a building **2.** *(verb)* to send something out

_____ **1.** Use a flashlight to _____ the light on the path.

_____ **2.** We need another _____ to hold up the roof.

> **odd 1.** *(adjective)* not what you are used to **2.** *(adjective)* cannot be divided evenly by two

_____ **3.** The number 11 is an _____ number.

_____ **4.** I find it _____ that you are here so early.

> **steer 1.** *(verb)* to move something in a certain direction **2.** *(noun)* a bull that is raised for meat

_____ **5.** Mom will _____ the car around the bus.

_____ **6.** The _____ won first prize at the state fair.

Shades of Meaning • Words That Describe Food

The word **lean** can mean "thin" or "without fat." It is often used to describe meat. Look at the chart for other words that can be used to tell about food. Think about how the words help you to imagine what a food is like.

lean	**Lean** meat does not have much fat.
spicy	**Spicy** foods have a strong flavor because there are many spices in them. They can make your mouth feel hot.
juicy	**Juicy** foods are full of juice and flavor.

Write the name of each food next to the word that best describes it.

> chili   hot pepper   skinless chicken
> peach   orange   sliced turkey

lean   1. _____   2. _____

spicy   3. _____   4. _____

juicy   5. _____   6. _____

Complete each sentence so that it makes sense. Use the word **lean**, **spicy**, *or* **juicy** *in your answer.*

7. My hands were a sweet, sticky mess after _____

_____.

8. My mouth was on fire after _____

_____.

9. When my brother wanted to lose weight, he exercised and

_____.

UNIT 13

Introducing the Words

Listen to this fairy tale about a girl who wanders into the home of three bears. Pay attention to the words in the color boxes. These are the words you will be learning in this unit.

Goldilocks and the Bear Family

(Fairy Tale)

Mama Bear, Papa Bear, and Little Bear lived in a big hollow tree in the forest. Papa Bear was an expert at cooking. One day, he made a very tasty soup.

"While we wait for our soup to cool," Mama Bear said, "let's walk to the post office and mail this letter." Mama Bear wrote an address on the letter. Little Bear found a stamp.

Soon after the bears left, a girl named Goldilocks walked down the forest path and right into their house!

"Ooh, soup," Goldilocks said in delight. She tasted from the first bowl. It was too hot. The second was too cold. The third was *just right,* and she ate the whole thing!

Then Goldilocks went into the living room, where she saw three books. The first book was too long. The second was too short. Goldilocks picked up the third book. "This book is *just long enough*."

Goldilocks read the first section of the book, but then it became difficult for her to stay awake. "I need to go relax," she yawned.

Goldilocks tried the beds. Papa Bear's bed was too hard. Mama Bear's was too soft. Little Bear's was *just perfect*.

When the bears got home, they could tell that someone had been there. They were not happy.

"Someone bent the pages of my book," Little Bear cried, "and that person ate my soup, too!"

Just then, the bears heard snoring. When they walked into the bedroom, Goldilocks woke up with a start.

She tried to make an excuse. "I was just watching the house while you were gone," she stammered.

The bears would not accept this. "You can't walk into someone's home without asking," they roared. "Please leave!"

Goldilocks dashed out quickly. She never bothered the bears again.

Word Meanings

You heard the words below in the passage on pages 142–143.
Read each word and its meaning. Write the word on the line
to complete the sentence.

1. accept
(verb)

When you **accept** something, you take
or receive it.

The company will _____
packages between 9:00 A.M. and 3:00 P.M.

2. address
(noun)

An **address** tells where a person or
business is located.

The _____ is 43 Grand Street,
Houston, TX.

(verb)

If you **address** people or groups, you speak to them.

Speak clearly and loudly when you

_____ the audience.

3. difficult
(adjective)

Something that is **difficult** is hard to do
or understand.

It is _____ to play chess well.

4. excuse
(noun)

An **excuse** is a reason that
explains a mistake.

My _____ for
being late is that I overslept.

(verb)

When you **excuse** another person,
you forgive the person.

Please _____ me for bumping into you!

5. expert
(noun)

An **expert** is someone who knows a lot about some special thing or does something really well.

Grandma Moses was an _____ painter.

6. hollow
(adjective)

Something **hollow** has a hole or an empty space inside.

The owl lives in a _____ tree trunk.

7. relax
(verb)

When you **relax**, you become less tense.

A back rub can _____ tight muscles.

8. section
(noun)

A **section** is part of a whole.

I never read the sports _____.

9. stamp
(noun)

A **stamp** is a small piece of printed paper that shows when postage is paid.

The letter was returned because it did not have a _____.

(verb)

If you **stamp** your foot, you put your foot down with force.

The camper will _____ out the fire so it doesn't spread.

10. whole
(adjective)

Something **whole** is complete. It has all its parts.

We could not eat the _____ pizza.

Match the Meaning

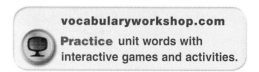
Choose the word from the box that matches the meaning in the clue. Write the word on the line.

accept	address	difficult	relax	whole

1. You write this information on an envelope. _____

2. You might do this if someone gives you a package.

_____

3. You try to do this on vacation. _____

4. You would eat this amount of a sandwich when you are hungry.

_____

5. You might describe juggling five balls this way. _____

excuse	expert	hollow	section	stamp

6. This might be what you tell a teacher if you don't do your

homework. _____

7. This person might teach a class. _____

8. This word can describe a cave or a straw. _____

9. This is what you put on an envelope to send a letter.

_____

10. This word names one part of a book or newspaper.

_____

Completing the Sentence

Choose the word from the box that best completes the
sentence. Write the word on the line.

accept	address	difficult	excuse	expert
hollow	relax	section	stamp	whole

1. It is not _____ to mail a package.

2. Here is how to send one like an _____.

3. Follow these steps, and there will be no _____
   for problems.

4. First, put the _____ set of objects in a large box.

5. Fill in any _____ spaces with crumpled newspaper.

6. Tape the box well to close it. Write the _____ on top.

7. Find the upper right _____ on the top of the box.

8. That is where the _____ or postage sticker will go.

9. Take the package to the post office, and _____.

10. In a few days, the person should receive and _____
    the package.

Words in Context

Read the restaurant review. Then write a sentence to answer each question below.

The Corner Diner

This reviewer cannot recommend The Corner Diner. There were many problems when I ate there. The hostess seated me in a section near the kitchen. It was difficult to get help from the waiter. I thought I would have to stamp my feet to get attention. The chef is an expert who has worked at many famous restaurants. Still, the food did not taste good. My piece of chicken was tough and dry. The dumplings were hollow instead of packed with meat and vegetables. I was disappointed with the whole dinner. If you want good food, go somewhere else. Next week, I will review The Fireside Restaurant.

1. Why do you think the reviewer is unhappy sitting near the kitchen?

_____

2. What is a good way to get someone's attention in a restaurant?

_____

3. What makes the chef at The Corner Diner an **expert**?

_____

4. Why does the reviewer complain about the **hollow** dumplings?

_____

Write Your Own

accept   address   excuse   relax

5. Write a sentence using a word in the box. _____

_____

Word Games

Find the word in the box that matches the clue.
Write each letter of the word on an answer blank.

accept	address	difficult	excuse	expert
hollow	relax	section	stamp	whole

1. put your foot down with force   _ _ _ _ _

2. empty   _ _ _ _ _ _

3. the total   _ _ _ _ _

4. hard   _ _ _ _ _ _ _ _ _

5. speak to   _ _ _ _ _ _ _

6. part of a whole   _ _ _ _ _ _ _

7. to take   _ _ _ _ _ _

8. a reason   _ _ _ _ _ _

9. a scientist   _ _ _ _ _ _

10. to make less tense   _ _ _ _ _

Look at the letters you wrote in the shaded column above.
Write them on the answer blanks below to answer the riddle.

What is in the middle of Italy?

_ _ _ _   _ _ _ _ _ _ _   _

UNIT 14

Introducing the Words

Listen to this article about train travel. Pay attention to the words in the color boxes. These are the words you will be learning in this unit.

One Great Way to Travel
(Magazine Article)

All aboard! All over the world, train travel is a major way for people to get around. Before there were trains, horse-drawn coaches and boats were the common ways for people to travel. Trains are much faster. They move on tracks made of steel rails. Trains also have railroad cars that attach to each other. This allows trains to carry many people at one time.

Today, we also have cars, buses, and planes for travel. However, the train is still a big part of our lives. The United States has a very large railway system. It has enough track to circle the earth five times! We are not the only country with these different ways of traveling. Other countries have similar ways to travel, too.

There are different kinds of trains. Some are commuter trains that people take to work every day. Commuter trains can fill up very quickly in the morning and early evening. These are the times when most people travel to

and from work. Trains can be so crowded that people have to
stand and hold onto a handle or a pole. Sometimes, there is
only room for a very slender person.

Another kind of train takes people long distances. These
trains sell only as many tickets as there are seats. That way,
each passenger has a seat. Many trains that travel long
distances have separate cars where people can eat and sleep.

Some people prepare for long train rides by packing books to
read or games to play. Other people like to spend the ride taking
in the sights. If this is what you choose to do, simply sit back
and admire the scenery. Your only task is to enjoy the ride!

Word Meanings

You heard the words below in the passage on pages 150–151. Read each word and its meaning. Write the word on the line to complete the sentence.

1. **admire**
(verb)

When you **admire** someone or something, you think highly of the person or thing.

The players _____ the coach because she is smart and kind.

2. **attach**
(verb)

If you **attach** something, you join or connect it.

Use tape to _____ the note to the door.

3. **handle**
(noun)

The **handle** of an object is the part you use to lift or hold it.

Pull hard on the _____ to open the door.

(verb)

If you **handle** a problem, you take care of it.

A plumber can _____ the problem of your leaky pipe.

4. **major**
(adjective)

Something **major** is important or great in size or number.

Heavy rain was a _____ cause of the flood.

5. **passenger**
(noun)

A **passenger** is someone who travels in a vehicle but is not the driver.

The _____ fell asleep in the car.

6. prepare
(verb)

To **prepare** is to get ready.

We will _____ for the birthday party by getting hats, candles, and cake.

7. separate
(verb)

When you **separate** things, you sort or set them apart.

Please _____ the dark and light clothes before putting them in the washing machine.

(adjective)

Separate objects are set apart. They are not joined.

The two sisters have _____ bedrooms.

8. similar
(adjective)

If two things are **similar**, they are alike or much the same.

It is hard to tell the two drinks apart because they have a _____ taste.

9. slender
(adjective)

A **slender** person or thing is thin.

The _____ tree branches snapped off in the storm.

10. task
(noun)

A **task** is a job to be done.

Each weekend during the fall, my _____ is to rake the leaves.

Match the Meaning

*Choose the word from the box that matches the meaning
in the clue. Write the word on the line.*

> **admire   attach   handle   prepare   separate**

1. You pull this to open a door. _____

2. You do this to a beautiful painting or a hero. _____

3. You can use glue or tape to do this. _____

4. You might do this to clothes when you pack them away for different

   seasons. _____

5. You should do this before a trip. _____

> **major   passenger   similar   slender   task**

6. This is how a person on a diet wants to look. _____

7. This is work such as cleaning or sweeping that needs to be done.

   _____

8. This word tells how two hats might look. _____

9. This is one of many people who sit in a car, bus, train, or plane.

   _____

10. This word describes a big or important part of something.

    _____

Completing the Sentence

Choose the word from the box that best completes the sentence. Write the word on the line.

admire	attach	handle	major	passenger
prepare	separate	similar	slender	task

1. A plane's emergency landing turned a _____ into a hero.

2. The woman did an important _____ that saved the day.

3. It was a good thing she read the manual to _____.

4. She was ready for the _____ job of opening the emergency back door.

5. A flight attendant did a _____ thing at the front of the plane.

6. The woman had to _____ a panel from the wall.

7. She could then turn the _____ to unlock the door.

8. Even though she was _____, she could lift the door.

9. Finally, she was able to _____ an escape slide.

10. All of the people on the plane _____ what she did.

Words in Context

Read the fantasy story. Then write a sentence to answer each question below.

The Space Trip

Anna was excited about her first ride into space. She climbed into the spaceship and took a seat. Another passenger was already on board. He had blue skin, four arms, and no hair. In a separate part of the ship sat a robot pilot. It said, "Prepare for launch! Fasten your seat belts!" The pilot then pulled a handle with three slender fingers. As the spaceship zoomed up, Anna's body pressed hard against the seat. Earth looked as small as a dot behind her. Soon the sky was black and full of stars. Anna leaned forward to admire the view. It was like nothing she had ever seen before.

1. Is the other **passenger** on the trip a person from Earth? Explain.

   _____

2. How do the passengers **prepare** for launch? _____

   _____

3. Which word in the story means "thin"? _____

   _____

4. Describe the view that Anna leans forward to **admire** during the trip.

   _____

Write Your Own

attach	major	similar	task

5. Write a sentence using a word in the box. _____

   _____

Word Games

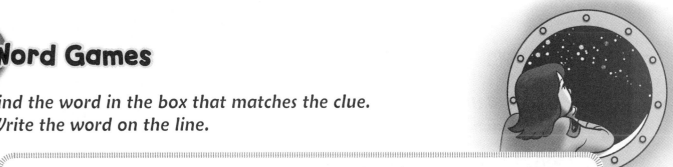

Find the word in the box that matches the clue.
Write the word on the line.

admire	attach	handle	major	passenger
prepare	separate	similar	slender	task

1. a thin pencil or person may look this way _____

2. get ready _____

3. the star of a movie gets this kind of part _____

4. something to do _____

5. what matching chairs are _____

6. doors, drawers, and windows all have this _____

7. a person riding on a train _____

8. glue can help things do this _____

9. look up to _____

10. things that are not together _____

Look at the words you wrote. Find them in the puzzle and circle them. You will find two of the words by looking down the columns.

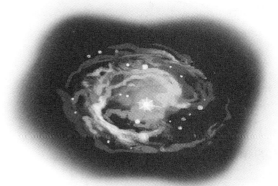

a	c	a	d	m	i	r	e	k	t
t	i	h	a	n	d	l	e	b	a
t	o	s	i	m	i	l	a	r	s
a	p	r	e	p	a	r	e	n	k
c	x	g	h	m	a	j	o	r	l
h	n	s	e	p	a	r	a	t	e
o	u	f	s	l	e	n	d	e	r
v	p	a	s	s	e	n	g	e	r

If you need help with a word, look it up in the **Glossary** at the back of this book.

Synonyms

*Circle the word that has almost the same meaning as the word in **dark print**. Write the word on the line.*

1. Please **stick** this label on the box.
   A. separate   **B.** prepare   **C.** attach   _____

2. The two hats I bought today are **alike**.
   A. similar   **B.** major   **C.** whole   _____

3. The hotel guests can **rest** by the pool.
   A. relax   **B.** separate   **C.** attach   _____

4. The first **job** is to rake the leaves.
   A. task   **B.** handle   **C.** excuse   _____

5. I will **plan** for the trip.
   A. address   **B.** prepare   **C.** admire   _____

Antonyms

*Circle the word that has almost the opposite meaning as the word in **dark print**. Write the word on the line.*

1. Lightning is a **minor** problem.
   A. hollow   **B.** major   **C.** similar   _____

2. Many people **dislike** the speaker.
   A. accept   **B.** prepare   **C.** admire   _____

3. The two teams will ride in the **same** buses.
   A. separate   **B.** slender   **C.** whole   _____

4. I **reject** your offer.
   A. stamp   **B.** relax   **C.** accept   _____

5. There was a **stuffed** piñata at the party.
   A. difficult   **B.** hollow   **C.** slender   _____

Classifying

Look at the words in the box. Write each word in the group in which it best fits. Use each word once.

address	difficult	expert	passenger
section	slender	stamp	whole

Words That Name Kinds of People

_____

_____

Words About the Mail

_____

_____

Words That Name Parts

_____

_____

Describing Words

_____

_____

Word Associations

*Choose the answer that best completes the sentence or answers the question. Pay attention to the word in **dark print**. Fill in the circle next to the answer.*

1. You might use a **handle** to
   - ○ open a door.
   - ○ cut a rope.
   - ○ write a story.

2. Where would you find a **passenger**?
   - ○ at the beach
   - ○ in a school
   - ○ on a train

3. It is **difficult** to
   - ○ lift a paper plate.
   - ○ climb a mountain.
   - ○ walk a dog.

4. You might eat a **whole** pizza if you are
   - ○ hungry.
   - ○ bored.
   - ○ tired.

5. How would you **prepare** dinner?
   - ○ by cooking it
   - ○ by eating it
   - ○ by cleaning it up

6. Which activity would most help a person **relax**?
   - ○ doing homework
   - ○ taking a nap
   - ○ cleaning the attic

7. You would **excuse** yourself from a party if you
   - ○ were having fun.
   - ○ felt sick.
   - ○ liked the music.

8. What is a **major** part of a sandwich?
   - ○ mustard
   - ○ lettuce
   - ○ bread

9. Which object is most **similar** to a pencil?
   - ○ paper
   - ○ eraser
   - ○ pen

10. Which object is **hollow**?
    - ○ plate
    - ○ spoon
    - ○ straw

Completing the Idea

Complete each sentence starter so that it makes sense.
*Pay attention to the word in **dark print**.*

1. I most **admire** _____

   _____

2. My favorite **section** of the neighborhood is _____

   _____

3. When I grow up, I want to be an **expert** in _____

   _____

4. I **prepare** each day for school because _____

   _____

5. The **task** I like least is _____

   _____

6. I find it **difficult** to _____

   _____

7. My **address** is _____

   _____

8. I **relax** when _____

   _____

9. A **major** part of my day is spent _____

   _____

10. The person I am most **similar** to is _____

    _____

Word Study • Context Clues

When you read, you may come across words that you do not know. Sometimes, the other words in the sentence can help you figure out the meaning of the word.

I was **absent** from school because I was sick.

In this sentence, the words **I was sick** give a clue to the meaning of the word **absent**.

Read each sentence. Underline the words that help you figure out the meaning of the word in dark print.

1. A **boulder** is a large, round rock.

2. I like to **munch** on peanuts and popcorn at the movies.

3. The sun will **disappear** behind the clouds.

4. We sat in a **cozy** spot by the fireplace.

5. Too much salt can **spoil** the soup.

Circle the word that best completes each sentence. Underline the words that helped you make your choice.

6. We stood on the (**stage, lake**) to sing our song.

7. The baby slept quietly in the (**leaf, cradle**).

8. Please buy some milk and apples at the (**market, cow**).

REVIEW UNITS 13–14

Shades of Meaning • Word Choice 3

You learned the meaning of **slender** on page 153. Look at the chart for words that are close in meaning to **slender**. Notice how the meanings of the words are alike and different.

slender	When someone or something is **slender**, that person or thing is thin but still healthy or strong.
skinny	A **skinny** object is very thin. A **skinny** person has little fat or muscle.
scrawny	When someone or something is **scrawny**, that person or thing may be weak from being too thin.

Write the word from the chart that best completes each sentence.

1. Dad is _____ because he gets a lot of exercise.

2. We used long, _____ sticks to roast marshmallows.

3. A flamingo is a pink bird with long, _____ legs.

4. This _____ chicken wing has hardly any meat on it.

5. Her arms are _____, but they can lift the heavy box.

6. When I found the puppy, it was _____ and dirty.

*Read each clue. Write the word that goes with each clue. Choose from **slender**, **skinny**, or **scrawny**.*

7. someone who is fit and in good shape _____

8. a stray, or homeless, cat _____

9. a healthy person who wants to build muscle _____

Match the Meaning

Choose the word that best matches the meaning.
Fill in the circle next to the word.

1. to make someone afraid
   ○ notice   ○ steer   ○ prepare   ○ frighten

2. to join one thing to another
   ○ attach   ○ separate   ○ address   ○ pitch

3. to receive something
   ○ scrape   ○ escape   ○ label   ○ accept

4. to get on
   ○ signal   ○ scatter   ○ board   ○ pack

5. to tell that something bad may happen
   ○ squeeze   ○ whisper   ○ carve   ○ warn

6. to shake
   ○ prove   ○ screech   ○ tremble   ○ seal

7. a group of animals
   ○ tool   ○ herd   ○ handle   ○ task

8. to jump forward
   ○ shiver   ○ leap   ○ soar   ○ beam

9. a large area without trees
   ○ soil   ○ stable   ○ field   ○ den

10. wet or moist
    ○ damp   ○ dangerous   ○ smooth   ○ calm

Completing the Sentence

Choose the word that best completes the sentence.
Fill in the circle next to the word.

11. Only 500 people live in the _____.
    ○ team   ○ village   ○ passenger   ○ whole

12. The traffic light helps bikers and drivers stay _____.
    ○ safe   ○ steady   ○ slender   ○ similar

13. My brother and I _____ different rocks.
    ○ plant   ○ cheer   ○ collect   ○ harm

14. I woke up at _____.
    ○ pain   ○ object   ○ dawn   ○ section

15. The insect I _____ most is the bee.
    ○ excuse   ○ fear   ○ relax   ○ sniff

16. I am _____ to open and unpack the box.
    ○ entire   ○ steep   ○ tender   ○ eager

17. My friend is _____ and always tells the truth.
    ○ honest   ○ difficult   ○ hollow   ○ tense

18. Seabirds _____ in the water for fish.
    ○ chew   ○ dive   ○ doubt   ○ lean

19. I am very _____ about snakes and turtles.
    ○ major   ○ fair   ○ proper   ○ curious

20. I know that a fly is an _____ because it has six legs.
    ○ insect   ○ island   ○ alarm   ○ enemy

Read this passage about a popular hobby, stamp collecting.
Then answer the questions on page 167.

U.S. stamps from the past

A Fun Hobby

Do you know what a *philatelist* is? It's a **stamp** collector. Stamp collecting has been around as long as there have been stamps. In the United States, the first stamps were sold in 1847. One had a picture of Benjamin Franklin. Another had a picture of George Washington. **Modern** stamps have all kinds of pictures, from movie stars to cartoons.

You do not have to be an **expert** to become a stamp collector. You can start by saving stamps you find on your family's mail. Then you can put them in a binder. You may pick a stamp because you **admire** the person or place shown on it. You can **select** stamps that you think are **odd**, or unusual. Each stamp is special in its own way. That is what makes collecting stamps such a fun hobby.

Choose the answer that best completes the sentence or answers the question. Fill in the circle next to the answer.

21. This passage is mostly about
- ○ the history of stamps.
- ○ the year 1847.
- ○ stamp collecting.

22. In this passage, the word **stamp** means
- ○ to mark something with ink.
- ○ to push your foot down hard.
- ○ a piece of paper put on mail.

23. The first U.S. stamps pictured
- ○ cartoons.
- ○ movie stars.
- ○ famous leaders.

24. What does the word **modern** mean?
- ○ past time
- ○ present time
- ○ future time

25. What is an **expert**?
- ○ someone who knows a lot
- ○ someone who makes stamps
- ○ someone who collects stamps

26. The word **admire** means
- ○ to collect something.
- ○ to think highly of.
- ○ to arrive somewhere.

27. What is another word for **select**?
- ○ pick
- ○ cross
- ○ stack

28. You can figure out that the author thinks stamp collecting is
- ○ only for adults.
- ○ fun and easy.
- ○ a difficult job.

29. In this passage, the word **odd** means
- ○ bright.
- ○ normal.
- ○ different.

30. The author most likely wrote this to
- ○ explain the reason we use stamps.
- ○ give facts about stamp collecting.
- ○ tell which stamps are the best.

In this glossary, each unit word is followed by its **pronunciation**. The pronunciation tells you how to say the word.

An **abbreviation** is a short way of writing a word. Here are some abbreviations you will find in this glossary.

n. noun   **adj.** adjective   **v.** verb   **adv.** adverb

Aa

accept (ak sept')
(v.) to take or receive something

address
1. (n.) (ad' res) where a person or business is located
2. (v.) (ə dres') to speak to a person or group

admire (ad mīr')
(v.) to think highly of a person or thing

agree (ə grē')
(v.) to think the same way someone else thinks

alarm (ə lärm')
(n.) something that wakes people or warns them of danger, such as a bell or a buzzer

arrive (ə rīv')
(v.) to reach the place you set out for

attach (ə tach')
(v.) to join or connect something

Bb

bare (bâr)
(adj.) not covered

beach (bēch)
(n.) a strip of land near the water that is usually sandy

beam (bēm)
1. (n.) a long, strong piece of wood or metal that holds up part of a building
2. (v.) to send something out over a long distance

bench (bench)
(n.) a long, narrow seat for a few people to sit on

board (bôrd)
1. (n.) a long, thin, flat piece of wood or plastic
2. (v.) to get on something

branch (branch)
(n.) a part of a tree that grows out from its trunk

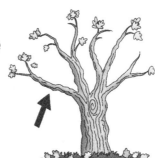

brave (brāv)
(adj.) having courage and not being afraid of danger

bridge (brij)
(*n.*) a structure above and across water or a road. People or cars can go over it to get to the other side.

bright (brīt)
1. (*adj.*) giving off a lot of light
2. (*adj.*) shiny

 **Cc**

calm (käm)
(*adj.*) quiet and still

carve (kärv)
(*v.*) to cut into something

center (sen' tər)
(*n.*) a place that is in the middle of something

cheer (chēr)
(*v.*) to yell or call out loudly

chew (chü)
(*v.*) to break into small pieces with teeth

clear (klēr)
1. (*adj.*) not cloudy or dark
2. (*adj.*) easy to see through

collect (kə lekt')
(*v.*) to gather things together

cross (krôs)
1. (*v.*) to go from one side to another
2. (*adj.*) angry or not pleased

crowd (kraùd)
(*n.*) a lot of people all together

curious (kyùr' ē əs)
(*adj.*) wanting to find out about something

Dd

damp (damp)
(*adj.*) a little wet or moist

dangerous (dān' jə rəs)
(*adj.*) not safe

dash (dash)
1. (*v.*) to move quickly
2. (*n.*) a small amount of something

dawn (dôn)
(*n.*) the time of day when the sun first comes up

deep (dēp)
(*adj.*) a long way down

den (den)
(*n.*) a place where some kinds of wild animals go to rest

difficult (dif' i kult)
(*adj.*) hard to do or understand

dive (dīv)
(*v.*) to go head first into water with your arms stretched out in front

doubt (daùt)
(*v.*) to be unsure about something

Ee

eager (ē′ gər)
(*adj.*) wanting to do something a lot

enemy (e′ nə mē)
(*n.*) an animal or person who doesn't like, or wants to harm, another animal or person

enormous (ē nôr′ məs)
(*adj.*) very big

entire (en tīr′)
(*adj.*) all of something

escape (es kāp′)
(*v.*) to get away from someone or something

evening (ēv′ niŋ)
(*n.*) the part of the day between afternoon and night

exactly (ig zakt′ lē)
(*adv.*) happening in the same way

excuse
1. (*n.*) (ek skūs′) a reason that explains a mistake
2. (*v.*) (ek skūz′) to forgive

expert (ek′ spûrt)
(*n.*) someone who knows a lot about some special thing or does something really well

Ff

fair (fâr)
1. (*adj.*) going by the rules and treating everyone the same
2. (*n.*) an outdoor place where people sell things. It is a place where people have fun.

famous (fa′ məs)
(*adj.*) well-known by many people

fear (fēr)
1. (*n.*) a feeling that danger is near or that something bad might happen
2. (*v.*) to be afraid of

feast (fēst)
(*n.*) a very large meal on a special day

field (fēld)
1. (*n.*) a grassy area where a game is played
2. (*n.*) a large area without trees

finally (fī′ nəl ē)
(*adv.*) at last

float (flōt)
(*v.*) to stay on top of water or in the air

flour (flaùr)
(*n.*) grain that is ground into powder and used for baking

forest (fôr′ est)
(*n.*) a large area with many trees

fresh (fresh)
1. (*adj.*) clean or new
2. (*adj.*) cool or refreshing

frighten (frī′ tən)
(*v.*) to scare someone

frown (fraůn)
1. (*v.*) to move your eyebrows together and wrinkle your forehead if unhappy or annoyed
2. (*n.*) an unhappy look on your face

Gg

gentle (jen′ təl)
(*adj.*) soft and mild

greedy (grē′ dē)
(*adj.*) wanting more of something than what is needed

Hh

handle (han′ dəl)
1. (*n.*) the part of something you use to lift or hold it
2. (*v.*) to take care of something

harm (härm)
(*v.*) to hurt

herd (hûrd)
(*n.*) a group of animals that may feed or travel together

hero (hir′ ō)
(*n.*) a person who is brave and does good things

hollow (häl′ ō)
(*adj.*) having a hole or an empty space inside

honest (än′ ist)
(*adj.*) when you tell the truth

hour (aůr)
(*n.*) a unit of time that is 60 minutes long

Ii

idea (ī dē′ ə)
(*n.*) a thought or a plan. An idea is something that you think of.

inn (in)
(*n.*) a small place where people can rent rooms and stay for the night

insect (in′ sekt)
(*n.*) a tiny animal with three main body parts, three pairs of legs, one or two pairs of wings, and no backbone. Ants and beetles are insects.

island (ī′ lənd)
(*n.*) land that has water all around it

GLOSSARY

GLOSSARY

Ll

label (lā′ bəl)
1. (n.) a sticker or tag fastened to something to tell more about it
2. (v.) to write something on a sticker or tag to tell more about it

leader (lē′ dər)
(n.) a person who shows people where to go or how to do something

lean (lēn)
1. (v.) to bend in a certain direction
2. (adj.) having little fat

leap (lēp)
(v.) to take a jump forward

Mm

major (mā′ jər)
(adj.) important or great in size or number

midnight (mid′ nīt)
(n.) 12 o'clock at night

modern (mod′ ərn)
(adj.) having something to do with the present time

Nn

nibble (ni′ bəl)
(v.) to eat with very small bites

notice (nō′ təs)
1. (v.) to see something or be aware of it for the first time
2. (n.) a sign put up for people to read

Oo

object (äb′ jəkt)
(n.) a thing you can see or touch

ocean (ō′ shən)
(n.) a very large area of salt water that covers almost three quarters of the earth

odd (äd)
1. (adj.) not what you are used to
2. (adj.) cannot be divided evenly by two

Pp

pack (pak)
1. (v.) to put things into a container, such as a bag, box, or suitcase
2. (n.) a group of something, such as animals, people, or things

pain (pān)
(n.) a feeling of hurt

pale (pāl)
(adj.) having little color

pass (pas)
1. (v.) to go by someone or something
2. (n.) a piece of paper that says the holder can do something or go some place

Permission to Park
LIC.# ATW 4137
The holder of this pass can park in the lot.

passenger (pas′ ən jər)
(n.) someone who travels in a vehicle but is not the driver

pitch (pich)
(v.) to throw

plant (plant)
1. (n.) a living thing that grows in soil or in water. It often has green leaves.
2. (v.) to put something, such as a seed, into the ground so that it can grow

prepare (pri pâr′)
(v.) to get ready

present (pre′ zənt)
1. (n.) something that is given to someone out of kindness
2. (adj.) in a place at a certain time

proper (präp′ ər)
(adj.) right or correct

prove (prüv)
(v.) to show that something is true

Rr

rainbow (rān′ bō)
(n.) long stripes of color that appear in the sky after a rainfall

relax (ri laks′)
(v.) to become less tense

Ss

safe (sāf)
1. (adj.) not in danger of being harmed or stolen
2. (n.) a strong box in which you can lock up money and other valuable things

scatter (ska′ tər)
(v.) to throw things over a large area

scrape (skrāp)
1. (v.) to rub something against a rough or sharp surface
2. (n.) a mark made on a surface by rubbing or scratching against something rough or sharp

screech (skrēch)
1. (n.) a loud, high sound
2. (v.) to make a loud sound

seal (sēl)
1. (n.) a sea animal that has thick fur and flippers. A seal can swim and live in cold places.
2. (v.) to close up tightly

GLOSSARY

search (sǝrch)
(v.) to look for or try to find

seashell (sē′ shel)
(n.) the shell of a sea animal such as an oyster or clam

section (sek′ shǝn)
(n.) part of a whole

select (si lekt′)
(v.) to pick something out

separate
1. (v.) (sep′ ǝ rāt) to sort or set apart
2. (adj.) (sep′ ǝr it) not joined

shiver (shi′ vǝr)
(v.) to shake quickly when cold or afraid

signal (sig′ nǝl)
(n.) anything that sends a message or a warning

similar (sim′ ǝ lǝr)
(adj.) alike; much the same

slender (slen′ dǝr)
(adj.) thin

smooth (smüͭh)
(adj.) not rough and bumpy, but flat and even

sniff (snif)
(v.) to take in air through your nose in short, quick breaths

snowstorm (snō′ stôrm)
(n.) a storm with a lot of snow

soar (sôr)
(v.) to fly very high in the air

soil (soil)
(n.) the dirt or earth that plants grow in

squeeze (skwēz)
(v.) to hold something tightly

stable (stā′ bǝl)
1. (n.) a building where horses are kept
2. (adj.) strong and not easily moved

stack (stak)
1. (n.) a neat pile of something
2. (v.) to pile one thing on top of another

stamp (stamp)
1. (n.) a small piece of printed paper that shows when postage is paid
2. (v.) to put your foot down with force

steady (ste′ dē)
(adj.) continuing and not changing much

steep (stēp)
(adj.) having a sharp slope; difficult to go up

steer (stēr)
1. (v.) to move something in a certain direction
2. (n.) a bull that is raised for meat

stream (strēm)
(n.) a body of flowing water that is narrow and shallow

Tt

task (task)
(*n.*) a job to be done

team (tēm)
(*n.*) a group of people who work together or play a sport together

tender (ten′ dər)
(*adj.*) soft and easy to cut

tense (tens)
(*adj.*) not able to relax

tiny (tī′ nē)
(*adj.*) very small

tool (tül)
(*n.*) a piece of equipment used to do a certain job

trail (trāl)
(*n.*) a path for people to follow, especially in the woods

travel (tra′ vəl)
(*v.*) to go from one place to another

tremble (trem′ bəl)
(*v.*) to shake a little from excitement or anger

Vv

village (vi′ lij)
(*n.*) a small town

Ww

warn (wôrn)
(*v.*) to tell someone about possible danger

wave (wāv)
1. (*v.*) to move your hand back and forth
2. (*n.*) something that looks like a long bump moving through the water in a lake or an ocean

weak (wēk)
(*adj.*) not strong

weekend (wēk′ end)
(*n.*) the two days of the week called Saturday and Sunday

whisper (hwis′ pər)
(*v.*) to speak in a very soft and quiet voice

whole (hōl)
(*adj.*) complete; having all its parts

wise (wīz)
(*adj.*) showing good sense and judgment

wonder (wən′ dər)
(*v.*) to be curious about something

worry (wər′ ē)
(*v.*) to feel that something bad may happen

GLOSSARY

Word List

The words below are taught in this book. The number after each word tells you the page where you can find the word.

accept, 144
address, 144
admire, 152
agree, 60
alarm, 78
arrive, 38
attach, 152

bare, 60
beach, 30
beam, 122
bench, 16
board, 108
branch, 8
brave, 8
bridge, 16
bright, 52

calm, 100
carve, 122
center, 30
cheer, 100
chew, 52
clear, 38
collect, 78
cross, 16
crowd, 16
curious, 108

damp, 78
dangerous, 108
dash, 8
dawn, 100

deep, 16
den, 122
difficult, 144
dive, 86
doubt, 108

eager, 108
enemy, 86
enormous, 38
entire, 100
escape, 130
evening, 8
exactly, 38
excuse, 144
expert, 145

fair, 100
famous, 60
fear, 109
feast, 60
field, 101
finally, 30
float, 38
flour, 52
forest, 52
fresh, 17
frighten, 86
frown, 17

gentle, 60
greedy, 8

handle, 152
harm, 101
herd, 86
hero, 61
hollow, 145
honest, 130
hour, 52

idea, 30
inn, 53
insect, 78
island, 53

label, 130
leader, 61
lean, 122
leap, 109

major, 152
midnight, 39
modern, 130

nibble, 53
notice, 61

object, 130
ocean, 30
odd, 122

pack, 86
pain, 101
pale, 53

pass, 9
passenger, 152
pitch, 131
plant, 78
prepare, 153
present, 9
proper, 123
prove, 87

rainbow, 39
relax, 145

safe, 79
scatter, 79
scrape, 123
screech, 109
seal, 87
search, 61
seashell, 31
section, 145
select, 131
separate, 153
shiver, 101
signal, 17
similar, 153
slender, 153
smooth, 87
sniff, 131
snowstorm, 39
soar, 87
soil, 79

squeeze, 109
stable, 131
stack, 31
stamp, 145
steady, 87
steep, 131
steer, 123
stream, 9

task, 153
team, 79
tender, 123
tense, 123
tiny, 31
tool, 79
trail, 9
travel, 17
tremble, 101

village, 109

warn, 53
wave, 31
weak, 61
weekend, 39
whisper, 39
whole, 145
wise, 9
wonder, 31
worry, 17